HBJ TREASURY OF LITERATURE

A MOST UNUSUAL SIGHT

SENIOR AUTHORS
ROGER C. FARR
DOROTHY S. STRICKLAND

AUTHORS
RICHARD F. ABRAHAMSON
ELLEN BOOTH CHURCH
BARBARA BOWEN COULTER
MARGARET A. GALLEGO
JUDITH L. IRVIN
KAREN KUTIPER
DONNA M. OGLE
TIMOTHY SHANAHAN
PATRICIA SMITH
JUNKO YOKOTA

SENIOR CONSULTANTS
BERNICE E. CULLINAN
W. DORSEY HAMMOND
ASA G. HILLIARD III

CONSULTANTS
ALONZO A. CRIM
ROLANDO R. HINOJOSA-SMITH
LEE BENNETT HOPKINS
ROBERT J. STERNBERG

HARCOURT BRACE & COMPANY
Orlando   Atlanta   Austin   Boston   San Francisco   Chicago   Dallas   New York
Toronto   London

ISBN 0-15-300423-1

6 7 8 9 10   048   96   95   94

Acknowledgments continue on page 349, which constitutes an extension of this copyright page.

Acknowledgments

For permission to reprint copyrighted material, grateful acknowledgment is made to the following sources:

Atheneum Publishers, an imprint of Macmillan Publishing Company: Cover illustration by Betsy Lewin from *Araminta's Paint Box* by Karen Ackerman. Illustration copyright © 1990 by Betsy Lewin.

Bantam Books, a division of Bantam Doubleday Dell Publishing Group, Inc.: Cover illustration by Neil Waldman from *A Horse Called Starfire* by Betty D. Boegehold. Illustration copyright © 1990 by Neil Waldman and Byron Preiss Visual Publications, Inc.

Bradbury Press, an affiliate of Macmillan, Inc.: From *Crinkleroot's Book of Animal Tracking* (Retitled: "Animal Tracking") by Jim Arnosky. Copyright © 1989 by Jim Arnosky.

Crown Publishers, Inc.: From pp. 34-55 in *The Secret of the Seal* (Retitled: "Kyo's Secret") by Deborah L. Davis, illustrated by Judy Labrasca. Text copyright © 1989 by Deborah L. Davis; illustrations copyright © 1989 by Judy Labrasca. From *Animal Fact/Animal Fable*. Text copyright © 1979 by Seymour Simon.

Delacorte Press, a division of Bantam Doubleday Dell Publishing Group, Inc.: Cover illustration by Denise Brunkus from *The Sly Spy* by Marjorie and Mitchell Sharmat. Illustration copyright © 1990 by Denise Brunkus.

Dell Books, a division of Bantam Doubleday Dell Publishing Group, Inc.: *The Pizza Monster* by Marjorie W. Sharmat and Mitchell Sharmat, illustrated by Denise Brunkus. Text copyright © 1989 by Marjorie Weinman Sharmat and Mitchell Sharmat; illustrations copyright © 1989 by Denise Brunkus.

Dial Books for Young Readers, a division of Penguin Books USA Inc.: *Bringing the Rain to Kapiti Plain* by Verna Aardema, illustrated by Beatriz Vidal. Text copyright © 1981 by Verna Aardema; illustrations copyright © 1981 by Beatriz Vidal.

Doubleday, a division of Bantam Doubleday Dell Publishing Group, Inc.: From *Why Can't I Fly?* by Ken Brown. Copyright © 1991 by Ken Brown.

Farrar, Straus and Giroux, Inc.: "Seal" from *Laughing Time* by William Jay Smith. Text copyright © 1955, 1957, 1980, 1990 by William Jay Smith.

Greenwillow Books, a division of William Morrow & Company, Inc.: Cover illustration by Jim Fowler from *The Secret Moose* by Jean Rogers. Illustration copyright © 1985 by Jim Fowler.

Harcourt Brace Jovanovich, Inc.: Cover illustration from *The Magic Fan* by Keith Baker. Copyright © 1989 by Keith Baker. Cover illustration by Margot Zemach from *The Chinese Mirror* by Mirra Ginsburg. Illustration copyright © 1988 by Margot Zemach. Pronunciation Key from *HBJ School Dictionary*, Third Edition. Text copyright © 1990 by Harcourt Brace Jovanovich, Inc.

HarperCollins Publishers: Cover illustration from *From Path to Highway: The Story of the Boston Post Road* by Gail Gibbons. Copyright © 1986 by Gail Gibbons. Published by Thomas Y. Crowell. *Sunken Treasure* by Gail Gibbons. Copyright © 1988 by Gail Gibbons. Published by Thomas Y. Crowell. "Tradition" from *Under the Sunday Tree* by Eloise Greenfield, paintings by Mr. Amos Ferguson. Text copyright © 1988 by Eloise Greenfield; paintings copyright © 1988 by Amos Ferguson.

Holiday House: From *Yellowstone Fires: Flames and Rebirth* by Dorothy Hinshaw Patent. Text copyright © 1990 by Dorothy Hinshaw Patent. All rights reserved.

Houghton Mifflin Company: *Buford the Little Bighorn* by Bill Peet. Copyright © 1967 by William Peet. Cover illustration from *No Such Things* by Bill Peet. Copyright © 1969 by William Peet. Illustrations from Bill Peet brochure produced by Houghton Mifflin Company. All rights reserved. *The Wreck of the Zephyr* by Chris Van Allsburg. Copyright © 1983 by Chris Van Allsburg.

Bobbi Katz: "Things To Do If You Are The Rain" from *Upside Down and Inside Out* by Bobbi Katz. Text copyright © 1982 by Bobbi Katz.

Alfred A. Knopf, Inc.: *Song and Dance Man* by Karen Ackerman, illustrated by Stephen Gammell. Text copyright © 1988 by Karen Ackerman; illustrations copyright © 1988 by Stephen Gammell. "A Day When Frogs Wear Shoes" from *More Stories Julian Tells* by Ann Cameron, illustrated by Ann Strugnell. Text copyright © 1986 by Ann Cameron; illustrations copyright © 1986 by Ann Strugnell. Cover illustration by Thomas B. Allen from *In Coal Country* by Judith Hendershot. Illustration copyright © 1987 by Thomas B. Allen.

Margaret K. McElderry Books, an imprint of Macmillan Publishing Company: "Cricket and Mountain Lion" from *Back in the Beforetime: Tales of the California Indians*, retold by Jane Louise Curry. Text copyright © 1987 by Jane Louise Curry.

William Morrow & Company, Inc.: "The Crow and the Pitcher" from *Belling the Cat and Other Aesop's Fables*, retold by Tom Paxton, illustrated by Robert Rayevsky. Text copyright © 1990 by Tom Paxton; illustrations copyright © 1990 by Robert Rayevsky. Cover illustration by Beth Peck from *The House on Maple Street* by Bonnie Pryor. Illustration copyright © 1987 by Beth Peck.

Pantheon Books, a division of Random House, Inc.: Cover illustration by Ann Strugnell from *The Stories Julian Tells* by Ann Cameron. Illustration copyright © 1981 by Ann Strugnell.

continued on page 349

HBJ TREASURY OF LITERATURE

Dear Reader,

Frogs wearing shoes, pizza monsters, boats that fly—each one of these is a most unusual sight! You might be a little surprised by all the wondrous things you'll see in the pages that follow.

You'll travel to some exciting places. Take a snowmobile ride and spend some time in an Inuit village. Walk an African plain where wild animals roam. Visit with a Russian family held together by strong traditions. Sing and dance with a grandfather who helps his grandchildren remember their heritage. Look through photographer William Muñoz's camera lens to share the drama of a major forest fire.

As you read the stories in this book, think about the special people you meet. As you share their experiences, you may begin to understand their points of view. Eloise Greenfield talks about how we learn from one another. She says:

> knowledge came from other lands
> Africans of long ago
> passed it down to us and so
> now we pass it on to you

The wonderful literature in this book was passed on to us, and we are proud to pass it on to you.

Sincerely,
The Authors

C O N T E N T S

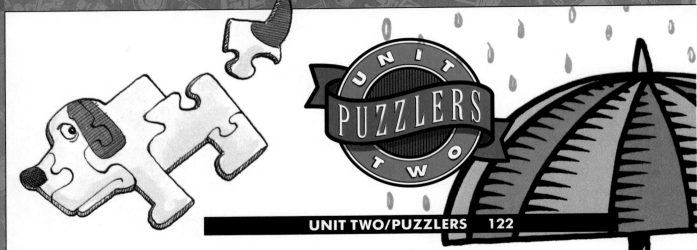

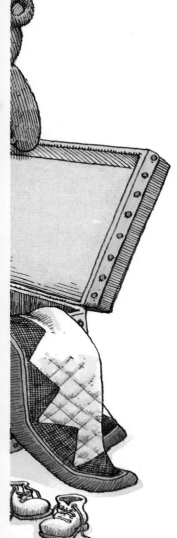

UNIT ONE

CREATURES

We can learn many things by watching and discovering. Whether we observe owls in a nearby field or seals in Alaska, noticing clues tells us a great deal about animals and the way they live. By looking at the sculptures of the Inuits of Canada, who call themselves "first people," we can learn about the animals in their environment. As you read the selections in this unit, watch for clues that could lead to some surprising discoveries about animals.

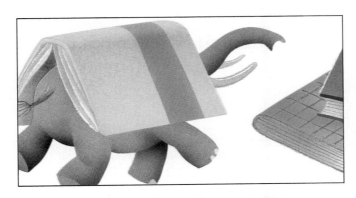

THE STORIES JULIAN TELLS

by Ann Cameron

Each of these six short stories about Julian, his friends, and his family will be sure to bring lots of smiles and laughs. They're as much fun to read silently as they are to read aloud. ALA NOTABLE BOOK, IRMA SIMONTON BLACK AWARD

HBJ LIBRARY BOOK

THE SECRET MOOSE

by Jean Rogers

This chapter book tells a story about Gerald and the moose he follows through the dense willows near his house. Boys and girls will enjoy the surprise ending.

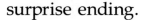

NO SUCH THINGS
by Bill Peet

This story in rhyme is a collection of some of Bill Peet's craziest creatures. It's an all-time favorite!

CHILDREN'S CHOICE

A HORSE CALLED STARFIRE
by Betty D. Boegehold

Friendship and trust develop between a horse and a young Native American boy. The bond between them changes the ways of Wolf Cub's tribe forever.   AWARD-WINNING AUTHOR

AMAZING WORLD OF NIGHT CREATURES
by Janet Craig

Creatures of the night, such as the kiwi, bat, and raccoon, come alive on each page. The pictures of nocturnal animals and the facts about them will hold everyone's attention.

TRACKING ANIMAL FRIENDS

Do you ever wonder how animals feel in hot weather? Have you ever found any signs that animals left behind? The following selections tell you some real and some not-so-real secrets about animals in the wild. The facts are mixed in with the fun.

C O N T E N T S

OWL MOON

by Jane Yolen

illustrated by John Schoenherr

CALDECOTT MEDAL
ALA NOTABLE BOOK

It was late one winter night,
long past my bedtime,
when Pa and I went owling.
There was no wind.
The trees stood still
as giant statues.
And the moon was so bright
the sky seemed to shine.
Somewhere behind us
a train whistle blew,
long and low,
like a sad, sad song.

I could hear it
through the woolen cap
Pa had pulled down
over my ears.
A farm dog answered the train,
and then a second dog
joined in.
They sang out,
trains and dogs,
for a real long time.
And when their voices
faded away
it was as quiet as a dream.
We walked on toward the woods,
Pa and I.

Our feet crunched
over the crisp snow
and little gray footprints
followed us.
Pa made a long shadow,
but mine was short and round.
I had to run after him
every now and then
to keep up,
and my short, round shadow
bumped after me.

But I never called out.
If you go owling
you have to be quiet,
that's what Pa always says.

I had been waiting
to go owling with Pa
for a long, long time.

We reached the line
of pine trees,
black and pointy
against the sky,
and Pa held up his hand.
I stopped right where I was
and waited.
He looked up,
as if searching the stars,
as if reading a map up there.

The moon made his face
into a silver mask.
Then he called:
"Whoo-whoo-who-who-who-whooooooo,"
the sound of a Great Horned Owl.
"Whoo-whoo-who-who-who-whooooooo."

Again he called out.
And then again.
After each call
he was silent
and for a moment we both listened.
But there was no answer.
Pa shrugged
and I shrugged.
I was not disappointed.
My brothers all said
sometimes there's an owl
and sometimes there isn't.

We walked on.
I could feel the cold,
as if someone's icy hand
was palm-down on my back.
And my nose
and the tops of my cheeks
felt cold and hot
at the same time.
But I never said a word.
If you go owling
you have to be quiet
and make your own heat.

We went into the woods.
The shadows
were the blackest things
I had ever seen.
They stained the white snow.
My mouth felt furry,
for the scarf over it
was wet and warm.
I didn't ask
what kinds of things
hide behind black trees
in the middle of the night.
When you go owling
you have to be brave.

Then we came to a clearing
in the dark woods.
The moon was high above us.
It seemed to fit
exactly
over the center of the clearing
and the snow below it
was whiter than the milk
in a cereal bowl.

I sighed
and Pa held up his hand
at the sound.
I put my mittens
over the scarf
over my mouth
and listened hard.
And then Pa called:
"*Whoo-whoo-who-who-who-whooooooo.*
Whoo-whoo-who-who-who-whooooooo."
I listened
and looked so hard
my ears hurt
and my eyes got cloudy
with the cold.
Pa raised his face
to call out again,
but before he could
open his mouth
an echo
came threading its way
through the trees.
"*Whoo-whoo-who-who-who-whooooooo.*"

Pa almost smiled.
Then he called back:
"Whoo-whoo-who-who-who-whooooooo,"
just as if he
and the owl
were talking about supper
or about the woods
or the moon
or the cold.
I took my mitten
off the scarf
off my mouth,
and I almost smiled, too.

The owl's call came closer,
from high up in the trees
on the edge of the meadow.
Nothing in the meadow moved.
All of a sudden
an owl shadow,
part of the big tree shadow,
lifted off
and flew right over us.
We watched silently
with heat in our mouths,
the heat of all those words
we had not spoken.
The shadow hooted again.

Pa turned on
his big flashlight
and caught the owl
just as it was landing
on a branch.

For one minute,
three minutes,
maybe even a hundred minutes,
we stared at one another.

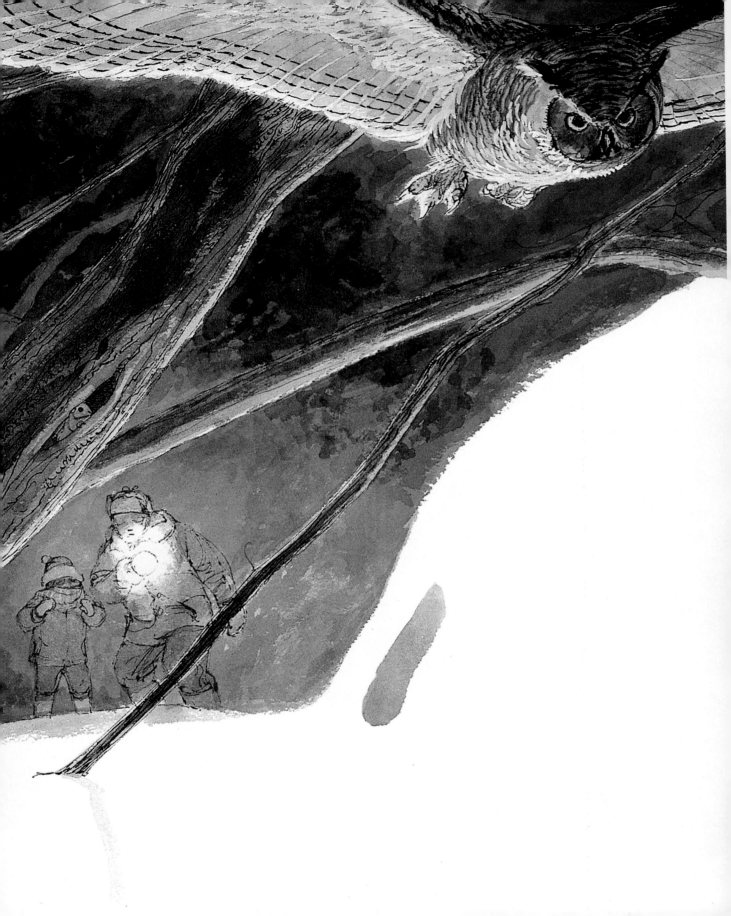

Then the owl
pumped its great wings
and lifted off the branch
like a shadow
without sound.
It flew back into the forest.
"Time to go home,"
Pa said to me.
I knew then I could talk,
I could even laugh out loud.
But I was a shadow
as we walked home.

When you go owling
you don't need words
or warm
or anything but hope.
That's what Pa says.
The kind of hope
that flies
on silent wings
under a shining
Owl Moon.

THINK IT OVER

1. Describe what the girl and her father did when they went owling.

2. According to the story, what is the most important thing to bring with you when you go owling? Share the reasons for your choice.

WRITE

The child tells us that "sometimes there's an owl and sometimes there isn't." Change the ending of the story to show how the child would feel if no owl had come. Write a new ending for the story and share it with your classmates.

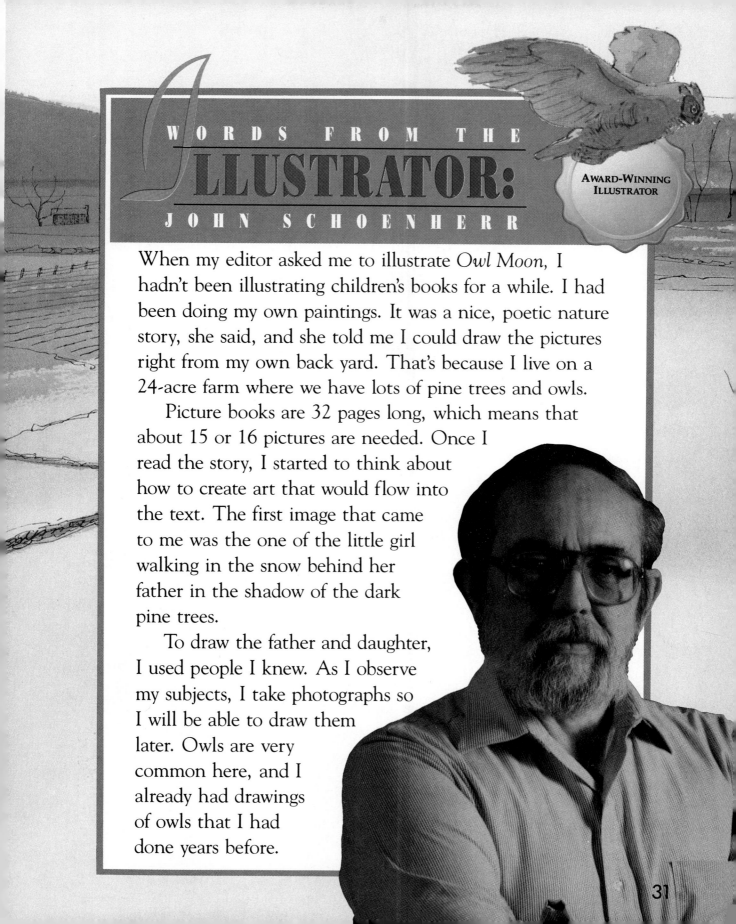

AWARD-WINNING
ILLUSTRATOR

When my editor asked me to illustrate *Owl Moon*, I hadn't been illustrating children's books for a while. I had been doing my own paintings. It was a nice, poetic nature story, she said, and she told me I could draw the pictures right from my own back yard. That's because I live on a 24-acre farm where we have lots of pine trees and owls.

Picture books are 32 pages long, which means that about 15 or 16 pictures are needed. Once I read the story, I started to think about how to create art that would flow into the text. The first image that came to me was the one of the little girl walking in the snow behind her father in the shadow of the dark pine trees.

To draw the father and daughter, I used people I knew. As I observe my subjects, I take photographs so I will be able to draw them later. Owls are very common here, and I already had drawings of owls that I had done years before.

Crinkleroot's
BOOK OF
ANimal TRACKiNG

JiM ARNOSKY

AWARD-WINNING
AUTHOR AND
ILLUSTRATOR

ANIMAL TRACKING

from *Crinkleroot's Book of Animal Tracking*

written and illustrated by

JIM ARNOSKY

Hello. You've been following Crinkleroot tracks. My name is Crinkleroot, and these are my tracks.

I can hear a fox turn in the forest, and spot a mole hole on a mountain. I can find an owl in the daytime.

When I walk about the forest, I leave signs that tell I've been around—my footprints. Animals leave marks and tracks that show where they have been and what they have been doing.

I can show you how I find signs of animals that live near me; then you can find signs of animals that live near you. One of the best places to look is around water.

Animals are attracted to streams and ponds, park fountains, and even damp patches of grass. There they find water to drink and food to eat.

This pond was created by beavers. Can you see the beaver signs?

Beavers have sharp teeth and can gnaw down a tree! Chewed-down trees and gnawed-off twigs are good beaver signs to look for.

Beavers create a pond by damming up a stream, using branches, sticks, and mud. A dam like this is a sure sign that beavers are living in the pond.

When a beaver fells a tree that is too heavy to drag to the water, it chews the tree into small logs and rolls each one into the pond. The beaver then pushes the floating log to wherever it is needed. Sometimes a beaver gets lucky, and the tree falls right into the pond.

Beavers use logs and chewed-off branches to build their homes, or lodges.

BEAVER

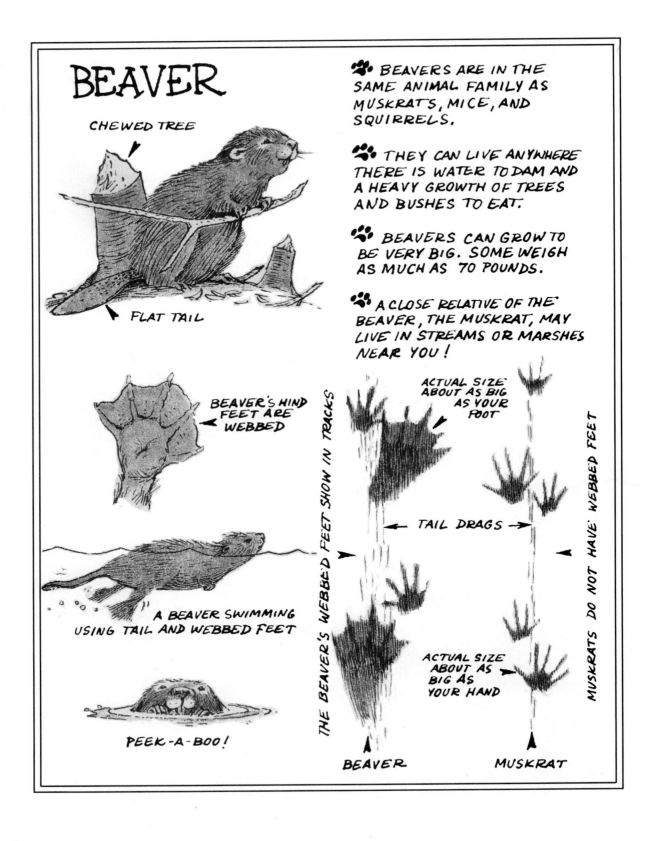

CHEWED TREE

FLAT TAIL

🐾 BEAVERS ARE IN THE SAME ANIMAL FAMILY AS MUSKRATS, MICE, AND SQUIRRELS.

🐾 THEY CAN LIVE ANYWHERE THERE IS WATER TO DAM AND A HEAVY GROWTH OF TREES AND BUSHES TO EAT.

🐾 BEAVERS CAN GROW TO BE VERY BIG. SOME WEIGH AS MUCH AS 70 POUNDS.

🐾 A CLOSE RELATIVE OF THE BEAVER, THE MUSKRAT, MAY LIVE IN STREAMS OR MARSHES NEAR YOU!

BEAVER'S HIND FEET ARE WEBBED

A BEAVER SWIMMING USING TAIL AND WEBBED FEET

PEEK-A-BOO!

THE BEAVER'S WEBBED FEET SHOW IN TRACKS

ACTUAL SIZE ABOUT AS BIG AS YOUR FOOT

TAIL DRAGS

ACTUAL SIZE ABOUT AS BIG AS YOUR HAND

MUSKRATS DO NOT HAVE WEBBED FEET

BEAVER

MUSKRAT

Beavers also eat the wood from trees they gnaw down. In autumn they gnaw off the small branches and store them on the bottom of the pond. In winter when the pond is frozen over, they will use these branches for food.

Let's wade around the shallow edges of the pond and look for other wildlife signs.

Here are webbed footprints, but these aren't beaver tracks. These tracks were made by an otter.

Otters are carefree critters. They play for hours, sliding down muddy spots on the pond bank and splashing into the water.

You may have seen otters sliding at the zoo.

OTTER

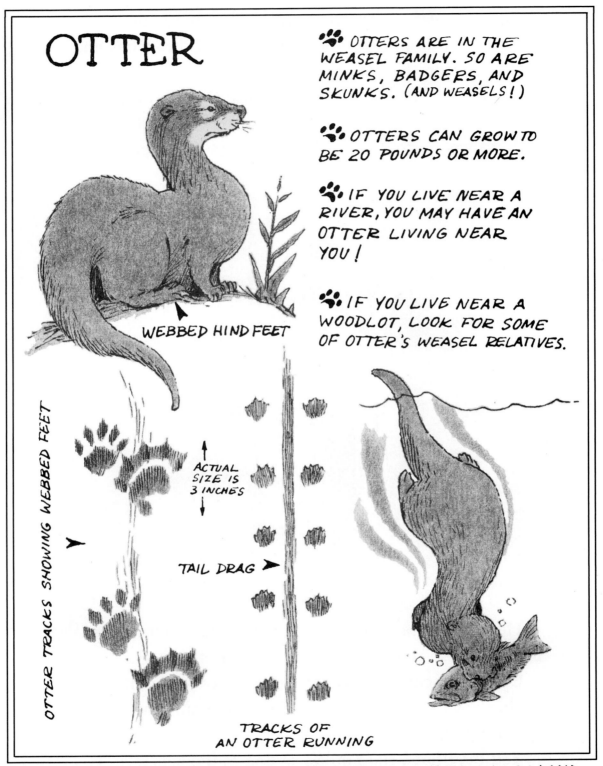

OTTERS ARE IN THE WEASEL FAMILY. SO ARE MINKS, BADGERS, AND SKUNKS. (AND WEASELS!)

OTTERS CAN GROW TO BE 20 POUNDS OR MORE.

IF YOU LIVE NEAR A RIVER, YOU MAY HAVE AN OTTER LIVING NEAR YOU!

IF YOU LIVE NEAR A WOODLOT, LOOK FOR SOME OF OTTER'S WEASEL RELATIVES.

WEBBED HIND FEET

OTTER TRACKS SHOWING WEBBED FEET

ACTUAL SIZE IS 3 INCHES

TAIL DRAG

TRACKS OF AN OTTER RUNNING

OTTERS ARE THE ONLY WEASELS MORE AT HOME IN WATER THAN ON LAND.

These footprints look like the prints of tiny human hands and feet. They were made by raccoons.

Raccoons eat anything they can catch or find. They even raid garbage cans. They come to the water to hunt for crayfish, frogs, snails, and freshwater clams.

Like many wild animals, raccoons are nocturnal. That means they are more active at night than during the day.

One night I watched a raccoon reach under the rocks in the shallow water of the pond. It was feeling for a crayfish hiding there.

The raccoon looked like a bandit in the moonlight.

RACCOON

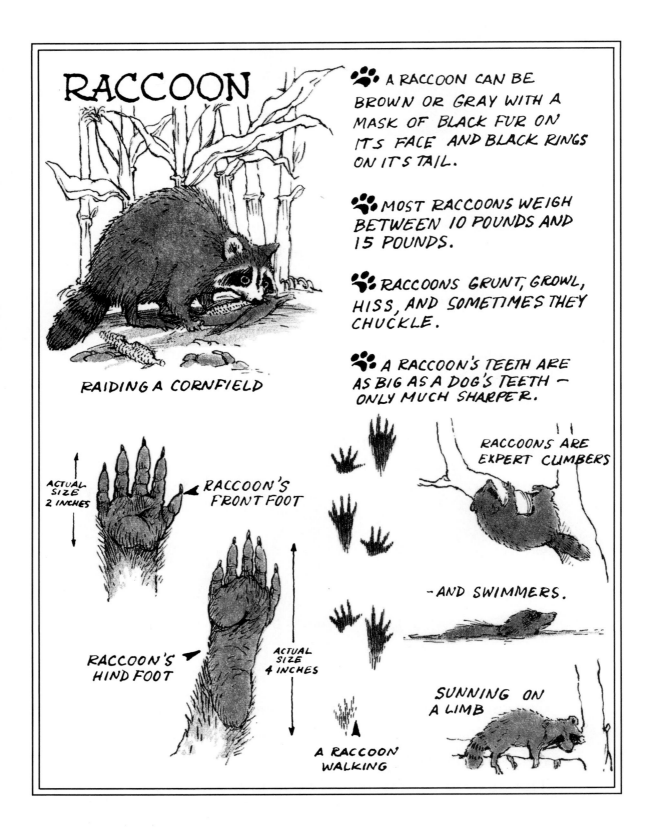

RAIDING A CORNFIELD

🐾 A RACCOON CAN BE BROWN OR GRAY WITH A MASK OF BLACK FUR ON IT'S FACE AND BLACK RINGS ON IT'S TAIL.

🐾 MOST RACCOONS WEIGH BETWEEN 10 POUNDS AND 15 POUNDS.

🐾 RACCOONS GRUNT, GROWL, HISS, AND SOMETIMES THEY CHUCKLE.

🐾 A RACCOON'S TEETH ARE AS BIG AS A DOG'S TEETH — ONLY MUCH SHARPER.

ACTUAL SIZE 2 INCHES

RACCOON'S FRONT FOOT

RACCOON'S HIND FOOT

ACTUAL SIZE 4 INCHES

A RACCOON WALKING

RACCOONS ARE EXPERT CLIMBERS

—AND SWIMMERS.

SUNNING ON A LIMB

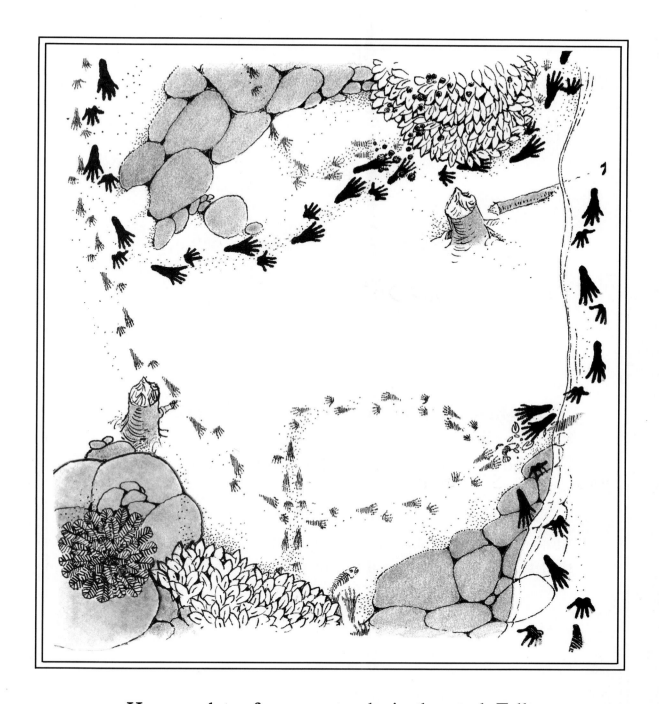

Here are lots of raccoon tracks in the mud. Follow them and see what they tell you. What did the big raccoons catch and eat? How many smaller raccoons were there?

Owls hunt at night. But I like to hunt for owls in the daytime. So can you. Here's how.

When an owl eats a mouse, it swallows it whole—tail and all.

The owl's stomach digests everything except the mouse bones and fur. The bones and fur form a ball that the owl coughs up and out onto the ground.

These balls of bones and fur are called owl pellets. They collect on the ground around trees where owls have been roosting. You can look for these pellets around the trees near your home. If you find some, look in the tree above for an owl sleeping the day away. That's how I find owls in the daytime.

Here are some owl pellets. Can you see an owl in this tree?

I've seen a lot of tracks here in the forest. I've even tracked fleas through the fur on a bear's back. But I can't seem to recognize these tracks next to my own.

Why, they must be yours.

Wherever you live, there are animals living near you. Look for the signs animals leave in parks and woodlots, on pavements and sidewalks, under trees, around streams and ponds, and in the snow. I can't promise you'll find any flea tracks, but you'll find something. And if you hear a soft swish in the night, go back to sleep. It's just a fox turning around somewhere in the forest.

THINK IT OVER

1. How does knowing about animal signs help you learn about animals?

2. Which animals that you read about are nocturnal?

3. Which animal do you think is the easiest to track? Why do you think so?

4. Would you like to go animal tracking with Crinkleroot? Explain why or why not.

WRITE

What animal signs can you look for where you live? Make a list.

A Day When Frogs Wear Shoes

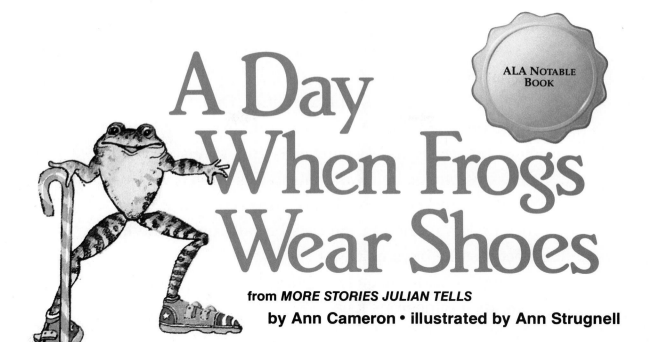

from *MORE STORIES JULIAN TELLS*

by Ann Cameron • illustrated by Ann Strugnell

My little brother, Huey, my best friend, Gloria, and I were sitting on our front steps. It was one of those hot summer days when everything stands still. We didn't know what to do. We were watching the grass grow. It didn't grow fast.

"You know something?" Gloria said. "This is a slow day."

"It's so slow the dogs don't bark," Huey said.

"It's so slow the flies don't fly," Gloria said.

"It's so slow the ice cream wouldn't melt," I said.

"If we had any ice cream," Huey said.

"But we don't," Gloria said.

We watched the grass some more.

"We better do something," I said.

"Like what?" Gloria asked.

"We could go visit Dad," Huey said.

"That's a *terrible* idea," I said.

"Why?" Huey asked. "I like visiting Dad."

My father has a shop about a mile from our house, where he fixes cars. Usually it is fun to visit him. If he has customers, he always introduces us as if we were important guests. If he doesn't have company, sometimes he lets us ride in the cars he puts up on the lift. Sometimes he buys us treats.

"Huey," I said, "usually, visiting Dad is a good idea. Today, it's a dangerous idea."

"Why?" Gloria said.

"Because we're bored," I said. "My dad hates it when people are bored. He says the world is so interesting nobody should ever be bored."

"I see," Gloria said, as if she didn't.

"So we'll go see him," Huey said, "and we just won't tell him we're bored. We're bored, but we won't tell him."

"Just so you remember that!" I said.

"Oh, I'll remember," Huey said.

Huey was wearing his angel look. When he has that look, you know he'll never remember anything.

Huey and I put on sweat bands. Gloria put on dark glasses. We started out.

The sun shined up at us from the sidewalks. Even the shadows on the street were hot as blankets.

Huey picked up a stick and scratched it along the sidewalk. "Oh, we're bored," he muttered. "Bored, bored, bored, bored, bored!"

"Huey!" I yelled. I wasn't bored anymore. I was nervous.

Finally we reached a sign:

RALPH'S CAR HOSPITAL
Punctures
Rust
Dents & Bashes
Bad Brakes
Bad Breaks
Unusual Complaints

That's my dad's sign. My dad is Ralph.

The parking lot had three cars in it. Dad was inside the shop, lifting the hood of another car. He didn't have any customers with him, so we didn't get to shake hands and feel like visiting mayors or congressmen.

"Hi, Dad," I said.

"Hi!" my dad said.

"We're—" Huey said.

I didn't trust Huey. I stepped on his foot.

"We're on a hike," I said.

"Well, nice of you to stop by," my father said. "If you want, you can stay awhile and help me."

"O.K.," we said.

So Huey sorted nuts and bolts. Gloria shined fenders with a rag. I held a new windshield wiper while my dad put it on a car window.

"Nice work, Huey and Julian and Gloria!" my dad said when we were done.

And then he sent us to the store across the street to buy paper cups and ice cubes and a can of frozen lemonade.

We mixed the lemonade in the shop. Then we sat out under the one tree by the side of the driveway and drank all of it.

"Good lemonade!" my father said. "So what are you kids going to do now?"

"Oh, hike!" I said.

"You know," my father answered, "I'm surprised at you kids picking a hot day like today for a hike. The ground is so hot. On a day like this, frogs wear shoes!"

"They do?" Huey said.

"Especially if they go hiking," my father said. "Of course, a lot of frogs, on a day like this, would stay home. So I wonder why you kids are hiking."

Sometimes my father notices too much. Then he gets yellow lights shining in his eyes, asking you to tell the whole truth. That's when I know to look at my feet.

"Oh," I said, "we *like* hiking."

But Gloria didn't know any better. She looked into my father's eyes. "Really," she said, "this wasn't a real hike. We came to see you."

"Oh, I see!" my father said, looking pleased.

"Because we were bored," Huey said.

My father jumped up so fast he tipped over his lemonade cup. "BORED!" my father yelled. "You were BORED?"

He picked up his cup and waved it in the air.

"And you think *I* don't get BORED?" my father roared, sprinkling out a few last drops of lemonade from his cup. "You think I don't get bored fixing cars when it's hot enough that frogs wear shoes?"

"'This is such an interesting world that nobody should ever be bored.' That's what you said," I reminded him.

"Last week," Huey added.

"Ummm," my father said. He got quiet.

He rubbed his hand over his mouth, the way he does when he's thinking.

"Why, of course," my father said, "I remember that. And it's the perfect, absolute truth. People absolutely SHOULD NOT get bored! However—" He paused. "It just happens that, sometimes, they do."

My father rubbed a line in the dirt with his shoe. He was thinking so hard I could see his thoughts standing by the tree and sitting on all the fenders of the cars.

"You know, if you three would kindly help me some more, I could leave a half hour early, and we could drive down by the river."

"We'll help," I said.

"Yes, and then we can look for frogs!" Huey said. So we stayed. We learned how to make a signal light blink. And afterward, on the way to the river, my dad bought us all ice cream cones. The ice cream did melt. Huey's melted all down the front of his shirt. It took him ten paper napkins and the river to clean up.

After Huey's shirt was clean, we took our shoes and socks off and went wading.

We looked for special rocks under the water—the ones that are beautiful until you take them out of the water, when they get dry and not so bright.

We found skipping stones and tried to see who could get the most skips from a stone.

We saw a school of minnows going as fast as they could to get away from us.

But we didn't see any frogs.

"If you want to see frogs," my father said, "you'll have to walk down the bank a ways and look hard."

So we decided to do that.

"Fine!" my father said. "But I'll stay here. I think I'm ready for a little nap."

"Naps are boring!" we said.

"Sometimes it's nice to be bored," my father said.

We left him with his eyes closed, sitting under a tree.

Huey saw the first frog. He almost stepped on it. It jumped into the water, and we ran after it.

Huey caught it and picked it up, and then I saw another one. I grabbed it.

It was slippery and strong and its body was cold, just like it wasn't the middle of summer. Then Gloria caught one too. The frogs wriggled in our hands, and we felt their hearts beating. Huey looked at their funny webbed feet.

"Their feet are good for swimming," he said, "but Dad is wrong. They don't wear shoes!"

"No way," Gloria said. "They sure don't wear shoes."

"Let's go tell him," I said.

We threw our frogs back into the river. They made little trails swimming away from us. And then we went back to my father.

He was sitting under the tree with his eyes shut. It looked like he hadn't moved an inch.

"We found frogs," Huey said, "and we've got news for you. They don't wear shoes!"

My father's eyes opened. "They don't?" he said.

"Well, I can't be right about everything. Dry your feet. Put your shoes on. It's time to go."

We all sat down to put on our shoes.

I pulled out a sock and put it on.

I stuck my foot into my shoe. My foot wouldn't go in.

I picked up the shoe and looked inside.

"Oh no!" I yelled.

There were two little eyes inside my shoe, looking out at me. Huey and Gloria grabbed their socks. All our shoes had frogs in them, every one.

"What did I tell you," my father said.

"You were right," we said. "It's a day when frogs wear shoes!"

THINK IT OVER

1. How did Dad help Julian, Huey, and Gloria when they were bored?

2. Why did Julian, Gloria, and Huey decide to visit Julian's father?

3. Was Julian correct when he said that visiting Dad was a dangerous idea? Tell why you think as you do.

4. What did Dad mean when he said that frogs wear shoes?

WRITE

Suppose you spent a hot summer day near a river. Write a postcard to a friend telling about what you did.

ANIMAL FACT/ ANIMAL FABLE

by Seymour Simon • illustrated by Manuel Garcia

Many of us like to watch animals. You may have a pet dog or cat. At times you may notice that your pet moves its tail differently when it's happy than when it's angry. After watching your pet for a long time, you can probably tell a great deal about what each kind of tail movement means.

But even if you watch animals closely, it is sometimes easy to mistake what is happening. For example, a bat flutters around in an odd way in the night sky. Some people may think that bats are blind and can't see where they are going.

If bats are really blind, that belief is true; it is a fact. But suppose the bat flies in that odd way for another reason, and is not really blind. Then the belief is a fable; it is not true.

On the following pages, we'll look at some common beliefs about animals. Guess if each belief is a fact or a fable; then turn the page to find the answer. You will also discover why scientists think the belief is a fact or a fable.

AWARD-WINNING
AUTHOR

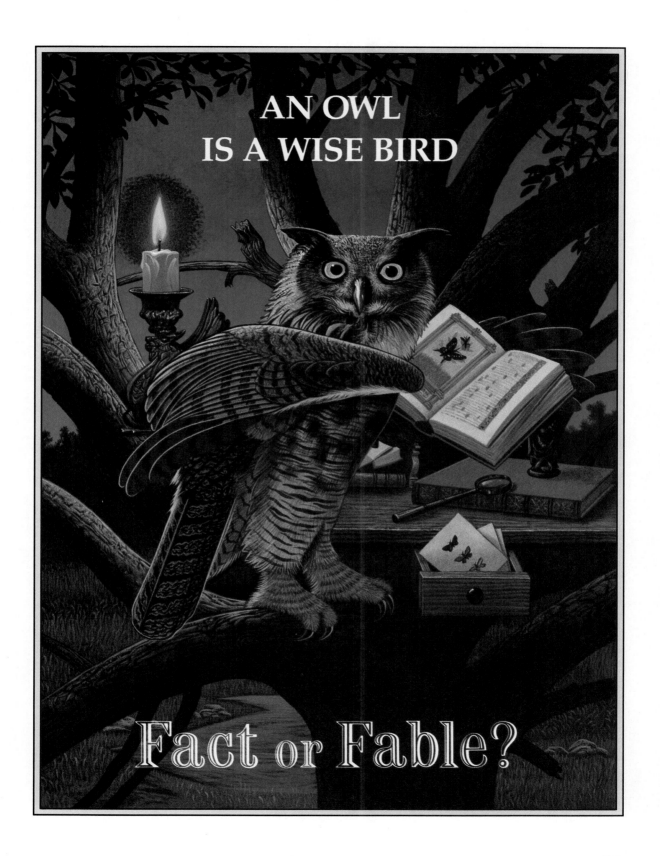

AN OWL
IS A WISE BIRD

Fact or Fable?

Fable

Some people think an owl looks wise because of its wide-open eyes. But for a bird its size, the owl has a tiny brain. If you say a person is as wise as an owl, you are saying he or she is a birdbrain!

An owl moves its whole head when it looks around. It never moves its eyes from side to side. Its eyes are very sharp. It can see even small objects, such as mice, that are very far away.

Fact

The archer fish shoots down insects that live near the banks of streams and ponds. When an archer sees an insect, it swims toward it. The archer raises its mouth close to the surface of the water. Then it squirts a spray of water.

The water drops hit the insect and the insect falls into the water. One swift gulp and the insect becomes a meal for the finned sharpshooter.

Fable

Raccoons sometimes dip their food into water before they eat, but they are not washing it. A raccoon's throat is not very large. It has trouble swallowing large pieces of food. Dipping food in water makes it softer and easier to swallow. When a raccoon finds a mushy piece of fruit, he doesn't wash it no matter how dirty it is. He just gulps it down right away.

THINK IT OVER

1. Think about the animals in the selection. What are the similarities and differences among them?

2. *Owls are not often seen.* Do you think this is a fact or a fable? Tell why you think as you do.

WRITE

Choose an animal and write your own fact or fable about it. Then write a paragraph explaining the fact or correcting the fable. Share it with your classmates.

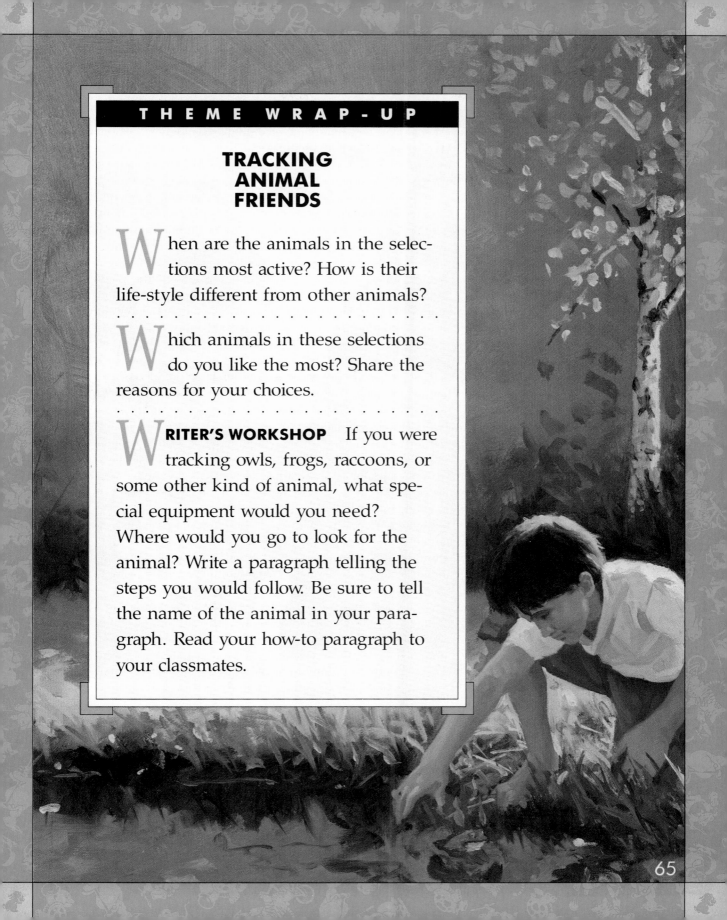

TRACKING ANIMAL FRIENDS

When are the animals in the selections most active? How is their life-style different from other animals?

. . . .

Which animals in these selections do you like the most? Share the reasons for your choices.

. . . .

WRITER'S WORKSHOP   If you were tracking owls, frogs, raccoons, or some other kind of animal, what special equipment would you need? Where would you go to look for the animal? Write a paragraph telling the steps you would follow. Be sure to tell the name of the animal in your paragraph. Read your how-to paragraph to your classmates.

65

BILL PEET'S CREATURES

Do you like to draw? One of the selections you are about to read started as a group of pictures. Then the artist decided to write a story about the creature he had drawn. The story became a book that was written and illustrated by the same person. In the pages that follow, Bill Peet tells how it all began.

C O N T E N T S

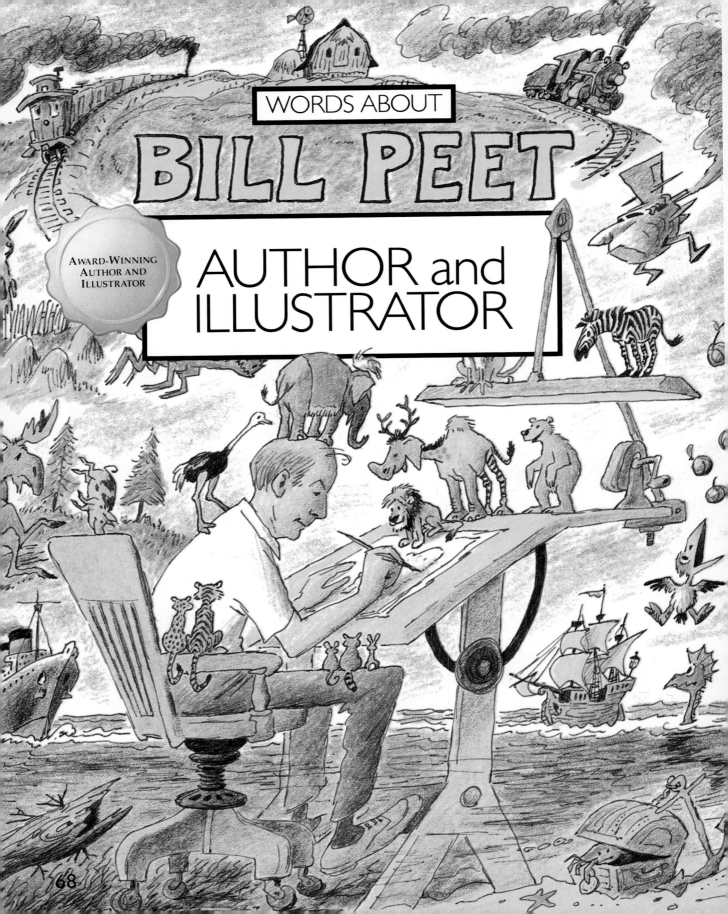

WORDS ABOUT

BILL PEET

AUTHOR and ILLUSTRATOR

AWARD-WINNING
AUTHOR AND
ILLUSTRATOR

"People sometimes ask me if I also illustrate
my own books. I tell them, I also write them.
I'm an illustrator first. I was always drawing,
from the time I was 4 or 5 years old."

Trains, pigs, dragons. When Bill Peet was a
child, he liked to draw them all. He
spent all his spare hours up in the
family's attic drawing away.

One reason he liked to spend
time upstairs, drawing by himself, was
that life wasn't very happy downstairs. His father had
gone away to fight during World War I and then failed
to rejoin his family in Indianapolis when the war
ended. Instead, Mr. Peet became a traveling salesman
who spent all his time on the road.

Money was tight in the house, so young Bill
took a job selling newspapers. He still had plenty of
time for fun, though. In the summer he would swim
with his friends, catching fish and tadpoles in the creek.
He liked to go down to the station and watch the trains
because he enjoyed drawing them. He also had fun on
his grandparents' farm playing with their dog, Towser.

Bill enjoyed reading books at the public library. His favorites were about big-game hunting and nature. He wanted to someday draw animals like the ones he saw on the pages.

Though he wanted to be an artist, times were hard and Bill thought he should take courses in high school that were practical. He didn't do very well and almost flunked out until he met an old friend who said, "Why aren't you taking art courses? You were always so good at that." Bill took his friend's advice, and his schoolwork went very well after that.

When he graduated, Bill went off to art school. The very first day, he saw a pretty girl named Margaret sitting in the front row. He knew she was the one for him, and they were married several years later. They've been married now for more than 50 years.

One of Bill Peet's most exciting moments as a young artist was winning a red ribbon at the Indiana State Fair Exhibition. Later he won other big prizes; but even with that success, Bill knew it would be hard to make a living as a painter at a time when it was very hard for people to find any jobs. He took a position drawing advertisements, hoping he could paint part-time.

Soon he got a better job offer, however. He was

chosen to join the team at Walt Disney Studios in California. It wasn't long before he was working on Donald Duck cartoons and then full-length features such as *Snow White and the Seven Dwarfs, Pinocchio,* and *Peter Pan.*

Walt Disney and his studio became very big and important. Bill Peet's job became more important, too. He worked for Disney for 27 years, but during all those years, Bill still wanted to be drawing his own pictures. He wanted to write and illustrate stories for children.

Some of his first efforts were made into short Disney films, such as *Lambert, the Sheepish Lion,* a story about a lion cub who is raised by a sheep. His first book without any Disney strings tied to it was *Hubert's Hair-Raising Adventure.* It is a story about an overly proud lion. After he'd had six books published, Peet left Walt Disney's studio for good. Then he started spending all of his time writing and illustrating books for children. *Chester the Worldly Pig, Pamela Camel,* and *Whingdingdilly* are some of the books he has had published. He's doing what he always dreamed of as a boy—drawing farms, trains, circuses, and animals.

BUFORD
THE LITTLE
BIGHORN

Written and Illustrated by BILL PEET

Buford was a scrawny little runt of a mountain sheep. Most of his growth had gone out the top of his head into a huge pair of horns. They went arching out over his back and on beyond him and still they weren't finished. Inch by inch and day by day they went curving onward while poor Buford worried. He was growing top-heavy and this could mean serious trouble to a mountain climber.

Like most bighorn sheep, Buford belonged to a flock that travelled about the mountaintops where it was all ups and downs with jagged rocks, narrow ledges, and steep cliffs. These sheep hardly ever worried about falling since they were all so nimble and sure-footed, that is everyone but the top-heavy Buford.

He came teetering and tottering along on shaky legs far behind all the others, and to the poor ram's dismay the top-heavy problem kept growing and growing. One day he discovered that his horns had taken a turn for the worse. They were heading his way!

"They're out to get me," thought Buford. "If they don't stop soon I'm sure to end up getting speared."

However, in a few months the horns grew on around him not even touching one hair of his hide, on past his legs, then on beyond his front feet to end up finally with a slight curl at the tips. The horn growing was finished but the damage was done. Now he must keep an eye on the cumbersome horns with every step for fear they might hook onto a ledge or catch in a cranny. Then there was always the danger of tripping over them.

"There's no doubt," grumbled the little ram, "but that these horns will be my downfall. One of these days they'll cause me to stumble and off the mountain I'll go."

And sure enough the horns did cause him to stumble and he toppled off a ledge to go tumbling down the mountainside.

Luckily for Buford, his horns hooked onto a snag of a spruce tree that stuck out from a crag. The horns had saved him from certain disaster. But then after all they were to blame for the fall.

The rest of the sheep were greatly alarmed by Buford's close call. From then on they pitched in to help. All the other rams took turns working as a team with two of them gripping his horns in their teeth while one gave Buford a big boost from below.

"How shameful," groaned the little bighorn, "to be so helpless and such a burden to my friends."

One morning as he was being hauled up a steep slope onto a flat table of rock, Buford decided he'd caused trouble enough.

"I can't let you help anymore," he said. "It's too much of a struggle, and besides it's not fair. So please go on your way and forget about me."

His friends stood around for a while looking sheepishly sad, and finally after wishing Buford the best of luck they went on their way. The unhappy little ram watched until the last of the sheep had disappeared over a distant ridge, then he turned his attention to the horns.

"I've got to get rid of these things," he muttered. "I'll knock them right off my head." And taking aim at a large boulder he went charging horns first like a battering ram. He hit with a jolting "Ker-wham!" to go tumbling backward, his head spinning from the shock.

When at last he was able to see straight, Buford discovered that the horns were still there as firmly rooted to his head as ever. "It's no use," he sighed, "these horns are mine for keeps. So I must figure out some way to live with them."

For a long time he stood on the edge of the bluff gazing into the valley far below. "It's mostly flat down there," thought Buford, "with no rocky ledges or steep drop-offs, so maybe that's where I belong. Then if I tripped on my horns I'd get no more than a good bump on the nose."

To get there he must make the hazardous trip down the steep rugged mountainside, which seemed impossible with the horns in the way. Just the same Buford was going, and choosing a place where the rocks formed narrow stair steps, he began the dangerous descent.

Whenever he came to a place that seemed the least bit too steep he stopped until he found a safer, easier way. Step by step he crept down the treacherous slope and by lunch time he had attracted a following of ravens and buzzards.

They expected the tottery, unsteady ram to tumble most any minute, and they were all set to peck up the pieces on the jagged rocks far below. "If these birds get a free meal," muttered Buford, "it won't be on me, not if I can help it."

All afternoon the ram picked his way carefully down
the steep mountainside, and without so much as one slip.
Just before sundown he had reached the foot of the last
rocky incline where the ground levelled off into a pine
forest. The danger was past, and for the first time in
his life Buford broke into a trot, leaving the miserable
ravens and buzzards perched in a pine.

It was such a relief to feel flat ground underfoot that
he kept right on trotting all the way through the forest
and out into a broad grassy meadow where someone was
shouting. "Halt! Halt I say! Not one more step! Do you
hear?"

A giant red bull followed by an army of bellowing

cattle came lumbering toward the terrified bighorn.
A beast from the forest could mean danger, and they
crowded in shoulder to shoulder all set to charge at a
word from their leader. After one close look the bull
scoffed, "It's nothing but a runt of a mountain sheep all
gone to horns. He's as harmless as a grasshopper."

With a few snorts of disgust the cattle ambled away
into the meadow, and as the bull turned to go he said,
"We'll not bother you, but there's no telling what the men
might do." Buford had heard about men. But right now
he was much too weary to worry about anything. He sank
to his knees, rolled over on his side, curled up in his horns,
and in seconds he was snoring. It had been a long day.

Next morning Buford was awakened by a sputtering, coughing, rickety old jeep that came lurching to a stop by a water trough. A man jumped from the jeep and climbed up the tower for a look at the windmill. It was barely turning and yet there was a lively breeze. As the man leaned in to inspect the machinery, the ram tiptoed quietly through the grass to slip in behind the nearest of the cattle.

There he remained stock still listening to the clanking of tools and the rusty squeaks of turning bolts. Pretty soon the windmill was whirling full tilt and the man went on his way. As the sputtering of the jeep faded into the distance the ram thought of a plan. After this he would keep well out of sight, and the huge herd of cattle would be his hideout.

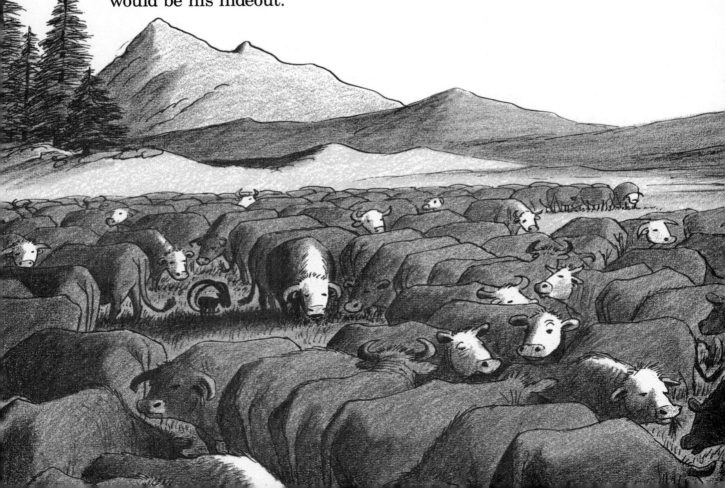

Men made the rounds of the cattle ranch every few days. Buford could hear their shouting and laughter. Sometimes they came in the jeep and sometimes on horseback, never suspecting that the little bighorn was their guest for the summer. He was always well hidden somewhere near the center of the great milling herd, grazing lazily on the tall tender grass.

After the grass had withered away to wiry brown stubble, the winter supply of hay was hauled in. There were heaping stacks of alfalfa on every part of the broad cattle range.

"This life is too easy, much too good to last," thought Buford. "Sooner or later something will happen."

And sure enough one day something *did* happen.

It was a day in November, bleak and cold, and the rolling pasture land was white with the first snowfall. Buford was having breakfast with the cattle at one of the haystacks when over the wintery stillness came the steady humming of an airplane. Gradually the humming grew into a furious roar and the ram jerked his head up for a look.

The plane was circling over the field like a great bird of prey closing in on some helpless victim down below. Suddenly it came swooping over the haystack and Buford caught a flashing glimpse of two men in the plane. They were staring at him! These men were hunters! It was bighorn hunting season!

By the time the plane came gliding down to land on its skis at the far end of the field, the ram was well on his way. He went galloping up through the pine forest, his horns leaving a deep-rutted trail as he went.

Buford was headed for the mountain tops where a blinding blizzard was howling. High up in the rocks the driving snow would wipe out his tracks. Then he might give the hunters the slip. But his chances of getting there were slim indeed.

In this one-sided game the hunters always won. And as the two men came trudging up the ram's trail with their high-powered rifles set for a shot, they were grinning. This was their lucky day. The great pair of horns would break all hunting records with plenty to spare, and these grand trophies would be theirs in a matter of minutes.

With time running short Buford didn't dare stop to figure out the best way up the mountain. When he reached the first rocky incline he went scrambling up, grabbing onto a ledge with his forefeet and pulling himself up by the chin. Then in a frenzy of kicks he heaved himself up and over. Quickly he struggled to his feet and was about to continue the climb when he let out a cry of despair. He had blundered head-on into a steep granite wall!

The wall reared straight up fifty feet into the air. Poor Buford was in a panic. Now he had to climb back down and try another way up if only there were time.

First he had to find out if the hunters were coming and he leaned out over the ledge to peer down into the forest. Buford leaned out too far. He lost his footing and off he went!

The ram hit the soft snow to go rolling head over heels down the slope, his huge horns whirling like cartwheels. He bounced off a stump, took one big flip in mid air, and then to Buford's amazement . . . .

. . . . he came down to land with all four feet planted squarely on his horns. And the horns were gliding over the slope exactly like skis, heading straight for the hunters crouching below. There was no chance for a shot. The men leaped from the path of the onrushing ram to go sprawling headlong into the snow. And in a flash their prize bighorn was gone.

There was no way of steering the runaway skis. Buford was too busy fighting to keep his balance. The ram tottered from side to side, which sent the horns zigzagging crazily around rocks and logs and between trees in one near miss after another. He was heading

back to the cattle ranch when the horns swerved sharply
to the right up over a ridge and down a long slope where
people were shouting. Lots of people!

He streaked past them so fast they were a blur of bright jackets and caps, and on down at the foot of the slope people were swarming like ants. There was no turning back! The bewildered bighorn went zooming straight into their midst to end up *Ker-floof!* in a great heap of snow.

At last Buford's luck had run out. He was trapped with no way to escape. The terrified ram couldn't bear to face the finish so he shut his eyes as the noisy crowd came closing in. Dozens of hands seized him by the horns to haul him out of the snow and he was lofted into the air.

As he was carried along, all at once the ram realized that this was a happy cheering crowd. These people weren't hunters, they were skiers like himself. This was a hero's welcome.

As suddenly as that Buford became the star attraction at the Little Big Pine winter resort. A special ski lift was rigged up for the remarkable ram, so there was no more struggling up steep slopes. It was all downhill from then on.

The little bighorn was surprisingly good for a beginner without any instruction. People came from such faraway places as Oslo, Innsbruck, and Banff to see Buford. However, his skill as a skier wasn't the only reason for all the big crowds. They had come to see the one and only skier ever to grow his own skis.

THINK IT OVER

1. Did you learn anything from reading about Buford? Explain your answer.

2. What kind of animal is Buford?

3. At the end of the story, Buford is a hero. What character traits does he have that make him a hero?

WRITE

What else could Buford have done to solve his problem? Write a friendly letter to Buford giving him suggestions.

WORDS FROM THE AUTHOR AND ILLUSTRATOR: BILL PEET

"When I draw, I start with a character. I doodle sketches of it, and then I stick it on my bulletin board and I look at it. Then, a story about that character comes to me. For instance, Huge Harold is a big, overgrown rabbit. I started thinking, 'What are the problems a rabbit like that might have?' Well, he couldn't hide for one thing. Then I drew his

parents, who were just regular size rabbits. That's when the story came to me.

"After I have the story figured out, I make a dummy, which is a practice version of the book. I send it to my editor, and the people at the publishing house make their own suggestions. Finally we agree on just what the story should be and which pictures we should use.

"Lots of people think I work in crayon, but actually it's ink and color pencil.

"When I'm not drawing, I'm reading my fan mail. One of the nicest letters said, 'DEAR BILL PEET, I WISH YOU WOULD WRITE A BOOK THAT WOULD NEVER END.'"

BILL PEET'S CREATURES

What special qualities does Buford possess? How do these qualities help him solve problems?

· ·

What do you think Buford and Huge Harold might talk about if they met?

· ·

WRITER'S WORKSHOP   Imagine that you had the chance to write to an author or illustrator. To whom would you write? What questions would you ask? Write a friendly letter to the author or illustrator of your choice. Be sure to include what interests you most about his or her work.

Remember that a letter needs a heading, a greeting, a body, a closing, and a signature.

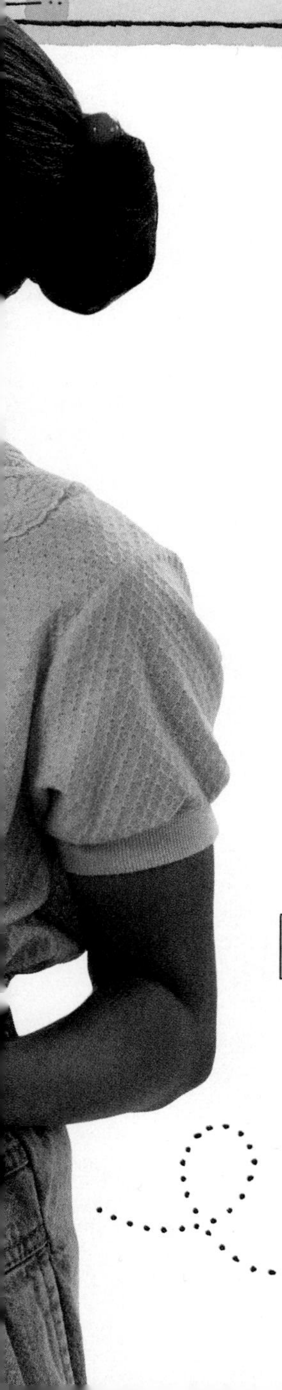

THEME

SECRET PETS

Have you ever owned a pet? Did you ever wish you had one? Think about what it would be like to have a secret pet. The selection and the poem that follow are about a kind of animal that is not usually someone's pet.

C O N T E N T S

KYO'S SECRET

from *The Secret of the Seal* • by Deborah Davis • illustrated by Judy Labrasca

Kyo's uncle George has come to visit, seeking a seal for a city zoo. Kyo[1] has a hard time keeping his uncle away from the spot on the bay where his secret friend is hidden under the ice.

Kyo couldn't fall asleep that night. When he heard deep snores from his uncle's bedroll on the floor across the room, Kyo slipped out of bed, went to the window, and parted the curtains.

The world outside was lit by an eerie silver glow. A big round disc of a moon hung in the sky. The snoring stopped, and Kyo heard rustling from George's bed. Turning, he saw the moonlight shining on his uncle's face.

Kyo quickly closed the curtains. The snoring resumed, and he put on his clothes as soundlessly as he could. Then he pulled on his boots and parka, eased the door open just enough for him to squeeze through, and found himself out in the nighttime glow.

He set out directly for Tooky's hole in the ice. Halfway there he remembered that if she had not been using the hole, it would have closed up, and he had not brought the pick. Still, he hurried on to their meeting place.

The hole was blocked by new ice, just as Kyo had expected. His throat tightened when he saw the frozen barrier. Sitting on the edge of the hole, he brought his heel down as hard as he could, but it bounced off the surface.

---

[1] Kyo [kē′·ō]

He leaned back, raising both feet high, and tried to smash the ice again. It didn't even crack. He considered jumping on the ice to break it open, but he knew that if he succeeded he'd likely drown.

"I'm not a seal," he said aloud. His words sounded small and lost in the strange night air. He lay on his belly and rubbed the surface of the ice with his mitten like he would wipe steam off his mother's mirror, hoping for a view of his friend below the surface.

"I don't know if you can hear me, Tooky," he said to the ice blocking his way, "but I'm doing my best to keep my uncle away from you. Keep checking this hole, Tooky, and when you see it open you'll know it's safe to come up and visit with me again. I don't know how long it will be, and I hope you don't give up. Please keep checking. I miss you!"

Kyo jumped up and started running back to his house. He stopped shortly, though, and ran back to the hole.

"I love you!" he called to his friend, and headed for the house again. As he ran the world darkened. He looked up to see the moon disappear behind a blanket of clouds. Snowflakes fell all around him. He slowed his pace as it got harder to see the path through the flurrying snow.

As Kyo reached his small dark house, the air cleared and the brightness returned. He turned to look out at the ice. Millions of freshly fallen flakes sparkled in the moonlight. Suddenly very sleepy, Kyo slipped inside the warm house and got into bed.

Smack smack! Thwack THWACK! Kyo opened his eyes hoping to see Tooky clapping her flippers, but instead he saw his mother making bread by the stove. He quickly glanced over at his uncle's sleeping place on the floor and sat up with a start when he saw it was empty.

"Mama, where's my uncle?" Kyo asked worriedly. Annawee[2] answered without turning from her dough.

"He's off seal hunting. He tried to wake you, but you slept as soundly as a baby. You can follow him after you eat. He didn't take his snowmobile, and he left good tracks in the snow that fell last night."

Tracks! Kyo thought. *I left tracks last night!* He'll see them.

Kyo jumped out of bed and pulled on his clothes.

"Can I take my breakfast with me, Mama? I want to go help my uncle. I don't want to miss anything." He made his eyes as big as he could, but he didn't have to worry about convincing her.

"I'm glad you want to help him. It's rare that we get to see Ahko.[3]" She wrapped generous portions of breakfast in a clean towel, which Kyo stuffed into his parka.

---

[2] Annawee [ă′·nă·wē]

[3] Ahko [ă′·kō]

"Goodbye!"

He ran out the door with his parka half open, pulling his mittens on his hands. He saw the tracks immediately: two sets of boots, big ones over little ones, following the path to Tooky's hole.

Kyo started to run down the path but changed his mind, going to the snowmobile instead. He jumped on the seat and sat for a moment, trying to remember how to start the engine. He turned the key, and the machine wheezed, coughed, and was silent. He tried again, and this time the whole thing shook and sputtered and growled—then was still. Kyo swung off the seat and kicked one of the runners.

"You have to start!" he shouted at the hulk of metal. Glancing at the house, Kyo saw Annawee's face appear briefly in the window. Before she reached the door Kyo was back on the snowmobile seat, turning the key. This time he remembered to turn the throttle.

The engine burst into its loud growl. Annawee's shouts were lost in the snowmobile roar as Kyo turned the throttle more and the machine lurched forward, pulling the sledge and cage away from the house and toward the great ice.

The world flew by. Thrilled by the speed, Kyo forgot for a moment that there was any danger, either to himself or to his friend at the end of the path. Rounding a protruding slab of ice, Kyo felt the machine lift slightly

off one runner. Scared that he might tip over, he slowed down a little.

George came into view. He was thrusting a pick into Tooky's old breathing hole to reopen it. Stunned by George's action and feeling helpless to stop him, Kyo let the snowmobile slide to a halt.

George finished hacking at the ice and looked up. He waved to Kyo, stepped back from the reopened hole, and picked up his rifle. Kyo jumped down and ran toward George, hoping that Tooky would not appear.

Just then her round head popped up in the hole.

"Don't come up!" Kyo tried to yell, but the words caught in his throat. Tooky slid onto the ice and began her awkward lope toward the boy.

"No!" he cried, and she stopped, confused. George lifted his gun and the movement caught the seal's eye. She whirled and bobbed quickly toward the hole.

George fired, dropped the gun, and raced toward the seal, who continued toward her escape, slowing as she reached it. George dove onto the ice and grabbed her tail just as her head dipped into the water.

"Kyo!" he yelled. "Come and help me pull her out! She'll die if she falls in."

Kyo reached them just seconds later. Together he and his uncle heaved and pulled the heavy, limp animal safely onto the ice.

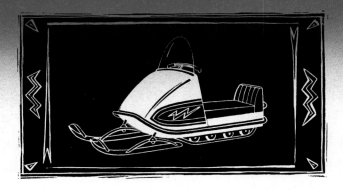

Kyo sank down beside the still form.

"Whew! That was close!" panted George. He too sat down beside the seal.

"She looks dead."

"Oh, no, Kyo. Remember, I told you that the darts only put the seal to sleep for a few hours. She hasn't been hurt at all."

Kyo wiped his eyes and nose on his sleeve. George glanced at the snowmobile and back to Kyo.

"You sure surprised me when you came flying down here on my machine. But then I could tell you were a smart boy. You learned quickly how to drive it."

Kyo was silent. He stared down at Tooky, wishing she would jump up and dive into the water before anyone could stop her.

"I'm not angry that you drove the snowmobile out here, Kyo. That was quick thinking. I'm just glad you didn't get hurt. You knew I'd find a seal here, didn't you? Or is there another boy with boots your size who walks out here often, sometimes with only the moon to light his way?"

Kyo ignored his uncle, who stood up and went to retrieve the gun. Kyo put his ear against Tooky and listened for her heartbeat. It was strong and even. Then he put his ear to her nose and felt her warm breath.

Satisfied that the seal was alive, Kyo sat up, his thoughts racing. He was afraid to tell his uncle that Tooky was a friend. George would never believe him. He would laugh at him or, worse, tell his parents and they would all have a good laugh at him during supper that night.

"Animals have a hard life," George had told him the day before. "They have to fight and struggle to survive." Maybe Tooky would be better off in the zoo after all, Kyo thought. Maybe she'd like having fish handed to her every day. Maybe fish are hard to find on her own. He wished he could just ask her, but he knew that even awake she could not answer him.

George drove the snowmobile up close to the seal, parking the cage beside her. "Give me a hand with her—say, Kyo, how did you know this seal was a female?"

"I've seen her before," Kyo said quietly. "And I won't help you put her in your rotten cage!" Kyo turned and ran off, away from his uncle and the sleeping seal and the settlement.

Shaking his head, George gently maneuvered the heavy seal into the cage. Then he started the engine and drove carefully back to the house.

Kyo walked in a wide circle that took him far out on the ice, then inland to the base of the mountains. He found a sunny spot out of the wind and sat down, took out his knife and stone, and began to carve.

Near dusk he stood up, stretched his legs, and started to climb. Stopping partway up the slope to catch his breath, he turned and faced the valley below. He picked out his own house among the others, all dark against the graying terrain. The snowmobile was parked near the house and George's figure moved beside it.

A shadow passed over Kyo, and he looked up to see a great snowy owl glide over his head. The huge bird's outspread wings beat slowly and firmly against the evening air.

Suddenly it dropped to the snow, talons first, then quickly lifted off with a small, white ball of fur wriggling in its grasp. The owl had caught its prey. It would eat that night.

Kyo realized he was hungry, too. Hours ago he'd consumed the food his mother had packed for him. He started down the mountainside.

A loud clamor of barking dogs greeted Kyo as he approached his home. He saw Tooky lying still in the cage. He hung his fingers on the wire and leaned his face against it.

George came out of the house just as Kyo turned to go inside. He mumbled a greeting to his uncle and brushed by him.

Annawee sat in her favorite chair, a kerosene lamp glowing on either side of her, needle in hand, cloth heaped in her lap. Kudlah[4] sat bent over a snowshoe frame, weaving narrow strips of leather, pulling them taut and securing them to the frame. They both looked up as Kyo came in and watched him slowly remove his parka.

"You look troubled, Kyo," said his father.

"I'm sad," he said, nodding. "And hungry."

Kudlah put down the snowshoe and went to the stove, where he ladled steaming soup into a bowl and set it on the table for the tired boy. He sat at the table with Kyo and watched him pour spoonfuls of soup into his mouth without pause. When the bowl was empty, Kyo asked for more. "Just half a bowl, please." Kudlah filled it and sat down again. When that was gone, too, Kyo pushed away the bowl and looked at his father.

---

[4] Kudlah [kō͞od′·lă]

"I saw a big white owl on the mountainside catch a mouse for its supper and I didn't feel sad. I was happy for the owl because it flew so smoothly and had no other way to get food." He stopped, but Kudlah just waited. Annawee had set down her needle. Her hands lay still in her lap.

"My uncle was happy to catch the seal today, but I'm not pleased for him at all. He says she'll be happier when someone gives her fish every day, but I wonder if she doesn't like to swim fast and catch her own."

No one spoke, and no one laughed.

"I've never seen a seal swim under water, but they sure are clumsy on land. They're really made to swim, aren't they? I bet they're graceful in the sea, like this!" Kyo picked up his spoon and made it swoop through the air.

"Whoosh . . . whoosh . . . whoosh!"

The door opened and George walked in, head hanging. Kudlah filled another bowl with soup and set it on the table for his brother-in-law. "Come eat, George. You must be hungry. Are you ready for the long trip back to the city tomorrow?"

George washed his hands and sat down heavily beside Kyo. "I am ready," he replied. "But the seal is not. She should have awakened by now. Something went wrong. She is dead."

Kyo jumped up and ran outside without stopping to put on his parka. The others stayed seated.

His heart pounding, Kyo unfastened the door to the cage and crawled inside, moving carefully around his friend. He bent to feel her breath on his ear. Nothing. He listened for a heartbeat and heard it, a little sluggish but steady.

Then he lifted his head again for a breath. It seemed like forever before he felt a gentle tickle against his skin. He waited, stock still, until he felt it again.

Sighing with relief, Kyo leaned back, stroking Tooky's head.

"Why won't you wake up?" He spoke to her still form. "I don't know how to help you, but first I want to get you out of this cage."

Kyo crawled out and stalked into the house.

"She isn't dead," he announced to the waiting adults, who looked surprised.

"Kyo," George said gently, "I know you're upset about this. But she isn't breathing—"

"She is, too!" Kyo interrupted. "You just have to be patient. You don't understand seals! Sometimes they don't breathe when they sleep. But she *will* wake up!" His voice shook, a little unsure, but he rushed on. "You have to help me move her. She will feel better when she's near the water."

"You have seen this animal before, Kyo?" asked Kudlah.

Kyo nodded his head.

"And she lets you get so close that you can watch how she breathes?"

"Yes," Kyo spoke quietly.

Kudlah wrinkled his brow pensively, then stood up.

"If the seal is dead, George, she'll be of no use to us. Her meat will be spoiled by the drug in your darts, and we must throw her back in the bay.

"And if she is alive"—he looked at Kyo—"perhaps the boy can wake her up."

Kudlah put on his parka and boots and left the house.

Annawee put aside her sewing and also got ready to go outside. George sat with his elbows on the table, head in his hands.

"Ahko!" Annawee spoke sharply to her brother. "Let us do what Kudlah says." George got up slowly and followed the others outside.

In the light of the rising moon the seal did indeed look dead. "We're going to help you now, Tooky," Kyo whispered through the wire.

As George climbed on the snowmobile, Kyo said to his father, "I want to move her with the dog team."

"All right," agreed Kudlah.

With four of them working, the sledge was unharnessed from the snowmobile and hitched up to the dogs in no time. Kudlah handed the traces to his son.

"You know how to do this, Kyo. George, here is your chance for a dogsled ride."

Eagerly Kyo stepped up onto the sledge. George got on, too, and sat down. Commanding the restless dogs to run, Kyo guided the sledge away from the house. He let the dogs go as fast as they wanted, and he looked back often to check on the seal. When the hole was in sight, Kyo slowed the team and brought the sledge to a halt.

"I have to unhitch the dogs so Tooky won't be scared when she wakes up," Kyo said to his uncle. He jumped down and began to free the sledge.

"The seal—what do you call her, Tooky?—won't wake up, Kyo. I'm afraid that the sleeping medicine was too strong for her." Kyo either didn't hear his uncle or ignored him. He unhitched the dogs from the sledge but kept them harnessed together.

"Here," Kyo said, holding out the traces to his uncle. "I need your help. Take the dogs to the house. Please."

Reluctantly George did as the boy asked. He led the dogs away from the sledge but stopped when he'd gone about fifty yards.

Kyo climbed back into the cage. Cradling the seal's head in his lap, he sang a song his mother used to sing to him.

Wake up, sleepyhead,
Wake up, dreaming one.
The sky is shining now—
Come outside and see the sun!

Three times Kyo sang the verse. On the fourth, Tooky opened her eyes and picked up her head. Kyo nudged her gently toward the cage door. The seal wriggled her body backward through the opening.

Seeing the animal leave the cage, the dogs and George rushed forward to prevent her escape. Kyo looked up to see the yapping dogs approaching and commanded them to halt. The dogs obeyed, and George stopped behind them.

On the ice now, Tooky sniffed in different directions as if to get her bearings. Kyo scrambled out of the cage, clapped his mittens together, and laughed. Then he dashed ahead, and Tooky skittered along behind him. George started after them again, but this time he stopped himself and watched them go.

When they reached Tooky's hole in the ice, Kyo sat by the edge and faced the seal. She put her nose close to his and gently brushed it with her whiskers.

Leaning back, Kyo broke the thin layer of newly formed ice easily with the heel of his boot. He stood up and watched Tooky dive into the sea. Then he turned from the hole to follow his uncle, who was already walking back to the house, dog traces in hand, leaving the empty cage behind.

THINK IT OVER

1. What are some of the reasons why Kyo doesn't tell anyone about Tooky?

2. According to Kyo's uncle George, why do some animals have a hard life?

3. If you were Kyo, what would you have said to Uncle George about Tooky? Why?

4. Do you think Kyo is ever lonely? Explain your answer.

WRITE

Why do you think Kyo chose the song he did when he sang to Tooky? Write a different song of your own that you think Tooky might like.

Seal

by William J. Smith
illustrated by Arnold Lobel

See how he dives
From the rocks with a zoom!
See how he darts
Through his watery room
Past crabs and eels
And green seaweed,
Past fluffs of sandy
Minnow feed!
See how he swims
With a swerve and a twist,
A flip of the flipper,
A flick of the wrist!
Quicksilver-quick,
Softer than spray,
Down he plunges
And sweeps away;
Before you can think,
Before you can utter
Words like "Dill pickle"
Or "Apple butter,"
Back up he swims
Past Sting Ray and Shark,
Out with a zoom,
A whoop, a bark;
Before you can say
Whatever you wish,
He plops at your side
With a mouthful of fish!

SECRET PETS

Kyo tries to keep the seal a secret from his uncle. Why does Kyo think he is doing the right thing?

· ·

What did you learn about the way seals move and live from the story and the poem you read?

· ·

WRITER'S WORKSHOP   Imagine that you have read about someone trying to capture a walrus or another wild animal. How would you feel? What would you do? Write a persuasive paragraph for a news editorial, telling what you think. Be sure to organize details in the order of their importance.

CONNECTIONS

INUIT SCULPTURE

Many Canadian Eskimos, or Inuits, known as the "first people," create beautiful soapstone sculptures. These carvings—made from a soft, heavy, grayish stone—reveal much about Inuit culture and about the animals that live in the Inuit's natural environment.

Their carvings often show the traditional way of life, such as scenes of people ice fishing or hunting. They also show seals, walruses, and other Arctic animals in lifelike poses.

■ Work with a group to have a First People Art Festival. Using clay, create your own version of Inuit sculpture, showing at least two animals. Then display your work for classmates to see and touch. You may want to create your own legend or tale to tell about the piece.

Soapstone sculpture is an important source of income for many Canadian Eskimos. Carvings made of the soft, heavy stone have become popular in the United States and Canada.

120

SPIN A WEB

Make a web like the one below of the animals you sculpted for the First People Art Festival. Fill in your web with facts you know about the animal and new information you learn from other sources. Share your web with classmates.

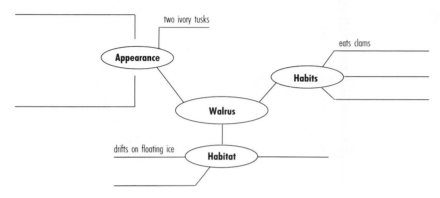

CREATURE FEATURE

Make a colorful poster about the animal you featured in your web. Include drawings or pictures of the animal and its home. Display your poster on a wall or bulletin board.

UNIT TWO

PUZZLERS

Listen, I know a secret!
Will you share
your secrets with me?
N. M. Bodecker

People have always been
puzzled by things they cannot
understand. They sometimes write
tales to explain what may have
happened. An African folktale tells
how a long drought was finally
ended. But no one has explained
what caused the people of the
ancient Mayan cities to disappear.
Finding solutions to such puzzles is
not always easy, but the selections in
this unit prove that it is often
possible.

PROBLEMS AND SOLUTIONS

126

BEING CLEVER

160

USING YOUR WITS

184

BOOKSHELF

$58 \div 2 = 29$

THE MAGIC FAN

written and illustrated by Keith Baker

Yoshi uses an unusual fan to help him solve the problems in his village. This beautiful book has magic of its own within the pages. AWARD-WINNING AUTHOR

HBJ LIBRARY BOOK

HERBIE JONES

by Suzy Kline

Herbie and his best friend come up with a few clever ideas to change their reading group. This book is just one in a series of the funny adventures Herbie experiences in third grade.

CHILDREN'S CHOICE

RENT A THIRD GRADER
by B. B. Hiller

A third-grade class learns a lesson in making money when they try to raise enough to pay for putting a retired police horse out to pasture. Some of the jobs the students take on don't always turn out as expected.

THE SLY SPY
by Marjorie and Mitchell Sharmat

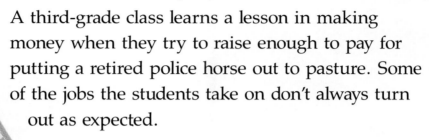

Olivia Sharp, Agent for Secrets, is solving cases again. This time Olivia is the one with the problem. Another agent is spoiling her business and she wants him stopped.

AWARD-WINNING AUTHORS

THE CHINESE MIRROR
by Mirra Ginsburg

How could a mirror cause so many problems? Learn the secret of a Chinese mirror in this Korean folktale. AWARD-WINNING AUTHOR

PROBLEMS AND SOLUTIONS

Sometimes people have to face problems. The problems are not always easy to solve. The selections that follow focus on problems involving nature and how those problems affect people.

C O N T E N T S

127

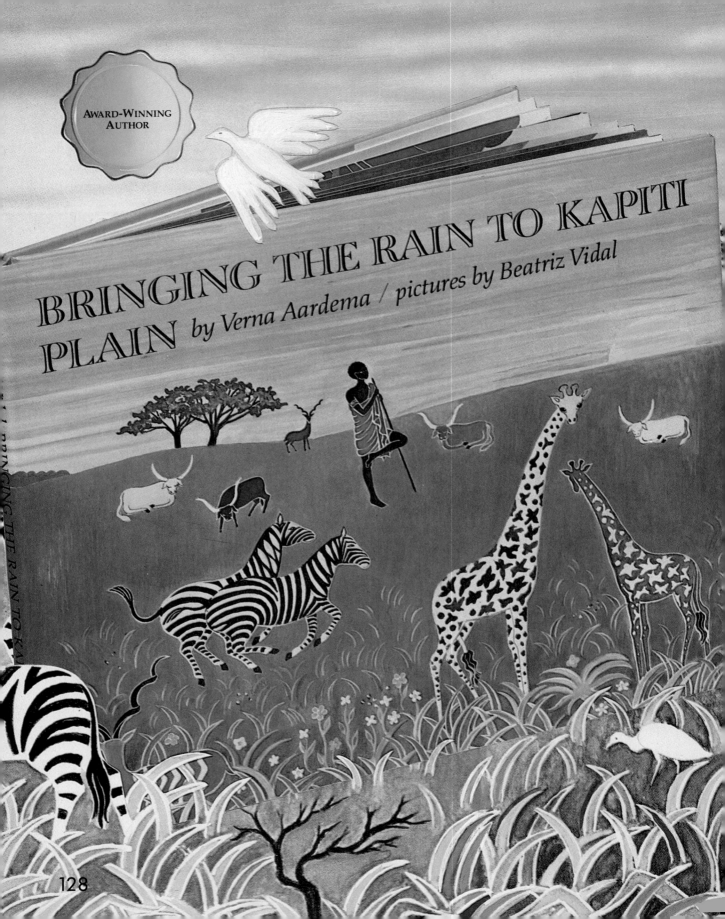

BRINGING THE RAIN TO KAPITI

PLAIN *by Verna Aardema* / *pictures by Beatriz Vidal*

This is the great
    Kapiti Plain,
All fresh and green
    from the African rains—
A sea of grass for the
    ground birds to nest in,
And patches of shade for
    wild creatures to rest in;
With acacia trees for
    giraffes to browse on,
And grass for the herdsmen
    to pasture their cows on.

But one year the rains
    were so very belated,
That all of the big wild
    creatures migrated.
Then Ki-pat helped to end
    that terrible drought—
And this story tells
    how it all came about!

129

This is the cloud,
    all heavy with rain,
That shadowed the ground
    on Kapiti Plain.

This is the grass,
    all brown and dead,
That needed the rain
    from the cloud overhead—
The big, black cloud,
    all heavy with rain,
That shadowed the ground
    on Kapiti Plain.

131

These are the cows,
    all hungry and dry,
Who mooed for the rain
    to fall from the sky;

To green-up the grass,
    all brown and dead,
That needed the rain
    from the cloud overhead—
The big, black cloud,
    all heavy with rain,
That shadowed the ground
    on Kapiti Plain.

This is Ki-pat,
    who watched his herd
As he stood on one leg,
    like the big stork bird;
Ki-pat, whose cows
    were so hungry and dry,
They mooed for the rain
    to fall from the sky;

To green-up the grass,
    all brown and dead,
That needed the rain
    from the cloud overhead—
The big, black cloud,
    all heavy with rain,
That shadowed the ground
    on Kapiti Plain.

This is the eagle
   who dropped a feather,
A feather that helped
   to change the weather.
It fell near Ki-pat,
   who watched his herd
As he stood on one leg,
   like the big stork bird;
Ki-pat, whose cows
   were so hungry and dry,
They mooed for the rain
   to fall from the sky;

To green-up the grass,
   all brown and dead,
That needed the rain
   from the cloud overhead—
The big, black cloud,
   all heavy with rain,
That shadowed the ground
   on Kapiti Plain.

This is the arrow
    Ki-pat put together,
With a slender stick
    and an eagle feather;
From the eagle who happened
    to drop a feather,
A feather that helped
    to change the weather.
It fell near Ki-pat,
    who watched his herd
As he stood on one leg,
    like the big stork bird;

Ki-pat, whose cows
    were so hungry and dry,
They mooed for the rain
    to fall from the sky;
To green-up the grass,
    all brown and dead,
That needed the rain
    from the cloud overhead—
The big, black cloud,
    all heavy with rain,
That shadowed the ground
    on Kapiti Plain.

135

This is the bow,
    so long and strong,
And strung with a string,
    a leather thong;
A bow for the arrow
    Ki-pat put together,
With a slender stick
    and an eagle feather;
From the eagle who happened
    to drop a feather,
A feather that helped
    to change the weather.

It fell near Ki-pat,
    who watched his herd
As he stood on one leg,
    like the big stork bird;
Ki-pat, whose cows
    were so hungry and dry,
They mooed for the rain
    to fall from the sky;
To green-up the grass,
    all brown and dead,
That needed the rain
    from the cloud overhead—
The big, black cloud,
    all heavy with rain,
That shadowed the ground
    on Kapiti Plain.

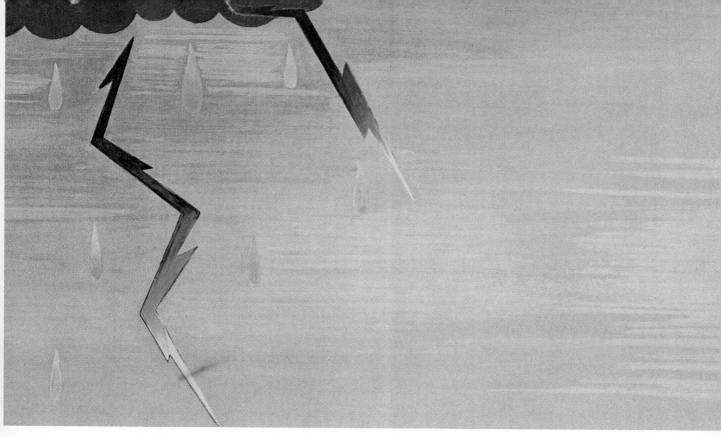

This was the shot
    that pierced the cloud
And loosed the rain
    with thunder LOUD!
A shot from the bow,
    so long and strong,
And strung with a string,
    a leather thong;
A bow for the arrow
    Ki-pat put together,
With a slender stick
    and an eagle feather;
From the eagle who happened
    to drop a feather,
A feather that helped
    to change the weather.

It fell near Ki-pat,
    who watched his herd
As he stood on one leg,
    like the big stork bird;
Ki-pat, whose cows
    were so hungry and dry,
They mooed for the rain
    to fall from the sky;
To green-up the grass,
    all brown and dead,
That needed the rain
    from the cloud overhead—
The big, black cloud,
    all heavy with rain,
That shadowed the ground
    on Kapiti Plain.

So the grass grew green,
  and the cattle fat!
And Ki-pat got a wife
  and a little Ki-pat—

Who tends the cows now,
  and shoots down the rain,
When black clouds shadow
  Kapiti Plain.

Think It Over

1. Why was the rain so important to Kapiti Plain?

2. On what continent does the story take place?

3. What caused the rain to fall, ending the drought?

Write

Ki-pat felt that he had to do something to end the drought. Write a paragraph about something you or someone you know had to do in order to solve a problem.

Things To Do
If You Are the Rain

by Bobbi Katz
illustrated by Jim Campbell

Be gentle.
Hide the edges of buildings.
Plip, plop in puddles.
Tap, tap, tap against the rooftops.
Sing your very own song!
Make the grass green.
Make the world smell special.
Race away on a gray cloud.
Sign your name with a rainbow.

Rain

by Myra Cohn Livingston

Weather

Anonymous

Summer rain
is soft and cool,
so I go barefoot
in a pool.

But winter rain
is cold, and pours,
so I must watch it
from indoors.

Whether the weather be fine
Or whether the weather be not,
Whether the weather be cold
Or whether the weather be hot,
We'll weather the weather
Whatever the weather,
Whether we like it or not.

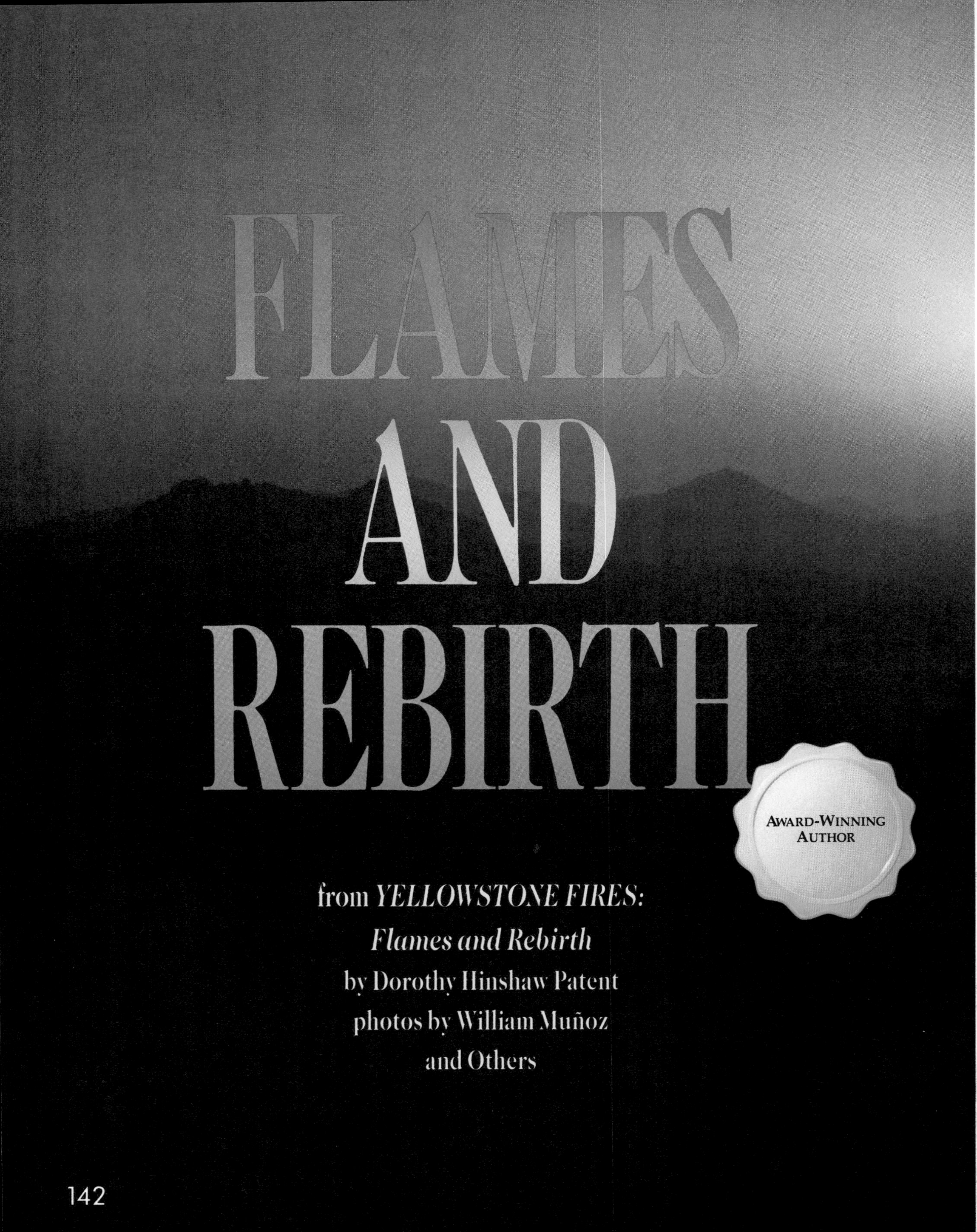

FLAMES AND REBIRTH

AWARD-WINNING AUTHOR

from *YELLOWSTONE FIRES: Flames and Rebirth*

by Dorothy Hinshaw Patent

photos by William Muñoz and Others

SETTING THE STAGE

In the summer of 1988, fires in Yellowstone National Park made news across the nation. Headlines screamed that the park had burned up, that nothing was left. Luckily, those stories weren't true. Yellowstone is alive and well. Much of the park did burn, but nature has been rebuilding. What really happened that summer? Why in Yellowstone? And what can we expect for the future of the park?

Background: Smoke from the fires often blocked out the sun.

Forests for Burning

Yellowstone will heal because it is used to fire. In our lives, we normally think in terms of a few years or at most a human lifetime. But the cycles of nature often are longer than that. In 1988, Yellowstone hadn't had huge fires since the early 1700s, although some large ones burned in the 1800s. The forests were ready to burn again.

Eighty percent of the park's trees are lodgepole pines—miles and miles of them. Lodgepoles grow quickly. But they don't live very long compared to some other trees. After about two hundred years, the trees in a lodgepole forest begin to die. The dead and dying trees are blown down in storms. As more and more trees fall, young ones grow up to take their place, and the floor of the forest keeps collecting wood from fallen trees.

In areas where lots of rain falls, the dead wood on the forest floor is attacked by fungus and bacteria which break it down. But in dry forests, like those of Yellowstone, most of the dead trees stay where they fall. Just like in a fireplace, this wood acts as fuel for fire. A lodgepole forest that is three hundred years old has so much dead wood that walking through it is difficult. There are logs to climb over everywhere.

Rain and Drought

Normally, the Yellowstone area gets most of its moisture in the wintertime, from snow. When spring comes, the snow melts, soaking the ground, and plants

grow. In normal years, some rain also comes to Yellowstone in June, July, and August.

It took hundreds of years to set the stage for the 1988 fires. Much of the forest grew for over two hundred years without really big fires, and the dead wood built up on the forest floor. Then, for six years in the 1980s, snowfall was light during the winter, making drought conditions build.

In April and May of 1988, much more than the normal amount of rain fell. This helped the small trees and other plants between the mature forest trees grow well. When June came, the park managers were not worried. They had no reason to suspect that June would only have 20 percent of its normal rainfall and that almost no rain would fall in early July. They didn't know that 1988 would turn out to be the driest summer ever recorded since the park was established 116 years earlier.

SHOULD WE PUT OUT FIRES?

Until 1972, all fires that started in national parks and that could be reached were fought. People saw fires as bad. After all, they killed trees and made ugly scars on the land. But as scientists learned more and more about nature, they realized that fire has its place. They learned that when dry northern forests go too long without fire, more and more nutrients are locked up in the dead and living trees. There aren't enough nutrients available for the trees to grow and stay healthy. It's as if the forests were starving.

Fire–A Part of Nature

When Yellowstone was founded over a hundred years ago, there were more open meadows than there are today. The lodgepole forests have been taking over the open land, leaving less room for grazing animals like elk to feed. Fires help maintain meadows by burning the small trees growing along their edges.

A Change of Policy

Once scientists understood that fire is an important natural force with healthy effects, they decided that not all fires should be fought after all. In 1972, a new policy began. If a fire was started by lightning in a national forest or a national park, it wasn't put out unless it caused forests, the needs of the timber industry, which cuts trees for wood and wood products, were also considered. The fires were watched closely. If they might become dangerous, they were stopped. Any fires caused by people were put out right away. The forest and park managers felt this new policy would help keep the parks and forests more natural.

Above:
The 1988 fires helped open up meadows in which elk could graze.

Background:
Lightning strikes cause many fires, but most burn out quickly.

YELLOWSTONE AFLAME

A number of fires started in Yellowstone and in the surrounding forests during June of 1988. The park itself lies at the center of a region called the "Yellowstone Ecosystem," or "Greater Yellowstone Area." Besides Yellowstone, the ecosystem includes Grand Teton National Park and the lands of several national forests. No one can hunt, cut trees for wood, or mine in a national park. But in the forests, these activities can take place.

Lightning sparked a fire on June 14 in the Storm Creek area of Custer National Forest north of the park. Officials decided to let it burn, since it was far from towns, homesites, or ranches. No one thought this fire would become destructive. But as the summer went on, it became one of the most dangerous of all, growing to more than 95,000 acres.

Left:
The fire approaches Old Faithful.

Background:
The North Fork Fire burns just a few miles south of Mammoth Hot Springs on September 10, the same day Mammoth was evacuated.

Fires started in the park itself as well. Many were allowed to burn, and most went out quickly by themselves before covering an acre. But by July 15 things began to look bad. The expected rainfall hadn't arrived, and the forests were very dry. About 8,000 acres in the park had burned. And winds were making the fires grow dangerously fast.

Trying to Stop the Fires

Less than a week later, on July 21, park officials decided to fight all fires in the park. By then, almost 17,000 acres had already burned. The next day, a cigarette left by a careless wood gatherer started a fire in the North Fork area of the Targhee National Forest just west of the park. Fire fighters began to fight it the same day. Meanwhile, in the northeast part of the park, two fires that started the second week in July joined to become the Clover-Mist Fire.

Unfortunately, the wind whipped up on July 23, two days after the decision to fight all fires. The combination of the wind and the dry conditions was too much for the fire fighters. The North Fork Fire, less than 30 acres when reported, grew to 500 acres before it was a day old, despite the fact that smoke jumpers—parachuting fire fighters—were sent in right away. The wind also carried bits of burning material such as pine cones called "firebrands," as far as a half mile in front of the fire. Officials didn't know it at the time, but the uncontrolled burning of Yellowstone had begun.

FIGHTING THE FIRES

As the fires burned, they threatened more than just Yellowstone's forests. The Clover-Mist and Storm Creek fires both came within a few miles of Cooke City and Silver Gate, Montana, two communities near the northeast corner of the park. Luckily, fire fighters stopped them from consuming the towns. The North Fork Fire threatened Canyon Village, inside the park. On August 24, five hundred tourists and employees were evacuated as the fire came within five miles of the area.

Uncontrollable Burning

The Yellowstone fires were awesome. No matter how hard they tried, humans could not stop them. The raging winds helped the flames race across the landscape. When firebrands hit dry timber, entire trees burst into flames. The trees were dry, and lots of dead wood lay on the forest floor. Trees killed by bark beetles stood in some areas, perfect fuel for flames. The rain didn't fall, and the trees were tinder-dry. These conditions are perfect for fires to crown. When that happens, the flames consume the entire tree. The tops, or crowns, of even the living trees become engulfed in flame. These are called "canopy fires," since they burn the branches that form a covering, or canopy, over the forest. Canopy fires are especially difficult to fight. The heat from the intense fire increases the wind, and the wind carries firebrands as far as two miles to unburned areas, starting still more fires.

Canopy fires can move very quickly, frustrating efforts to stop them. And firebrands can start fires behind the fire fighters, making their work especially dangerous. They could become quickly surrounded by flames and trapped.

Background: The canopy fires of 1988 were an awesome sight.

Above:
A burned marsh in fall 1988.

Background:
Meadows as well as forests burned in 1988.

AFTERMATH

Snow and rain stopped the worst of the fires in September. But here and there, fires smoldered and occasionally flamed up until November. By the time it was all over, eight huge fires had covered almost half of the park. The northwestern corner was hardest hit. But the southeast and northeast corners were also badly burned. Altogether, eleven major fires had burned in the Greater Yellowstone Area, fought by 9,500 fire fighters. In the wake of the fires, officials decided temporarily to fight all fires in national parks and forests until a new policy that coordinated fire management plans in parks and the surrounding national forests could be worked out.

How Much Burned?

Now it was time to see how much damage the fires had really caused. Television and newspaper stories made it sound as if Yellowstone was destroyed. But it wasn't. Many of the fires had not crowned and become canopy fires. They had just burned along the forest floor and not killed the trees. Other fires had burned over meadows and sagebrush.

Park researchers looked at the soil to see if plant roots and seeds had been killed. Fortunately, even in the worst burn areas, the roots of bushes were still alive below the ground. Lodgepole cones opened by the fire had scattered seeds all over the forest floor. They would grow to form the new forest.

Fire and Wildlife

Many people worried about the park animals during the fires. Would they be burned? It is difficult to count animals killed in fires, especially small ones. But the bodies of fewer than three hundred large animals, mostly elk, were found out of the thousands that roam the park. When the fire approached, bison, elk, deer, and pronghorn just moved away. Throughout the park, animals grazed near the fires. They were more disturbed by the noisy helicopters that flew overhead than by the flames.

Right:
Animals like the coyote benefited from the fires.

Background:
Yellowstone bison like these will be healthier after eating the nutritious grass that follows fire.

Some birds benefited during the fires. They hunted for food near the edges of the fires, feeding on small animals that were escaping. Young bald eagles had already flown from their nests before the fires threatened them, so they escaped. One osprey nest was burned before the young could fly.

THE FUTURE

Signs of renewal were already clear in the spring of 1989. Twenty kinds of grasses sprouted on the burned forest floor, mixed with flowers such as delicate shooting stars. The burned meadows grew more vigorously than before, with a healthy, deep green glow, nourished by the nitrogen and other nutrients released by the fires. The new growth is not only healthy and green, it actually contains more nutrients for the animals like elk that eat it. Grazers prefer the grass and other plants in recently burned areas, and it makes them healthier than grass in unburned meadows.

The lodgepole pine seeds covering the forest floor also began to grow into new trees that year. They were tiny and difficult to see, but they were there. By the end of the growing season, they had reached an inch and a half in height. Between the new seedlings, the roots of bushes and shrubs had sent up new growth, giving the blackened forest some greenery.

burned, the weak trees will begin to die and fall to the forest floor. The cycle will begin to turn back toward its beginning, with fuel for future forests starting to build up underneath the trees. And later on, probably sometime during the twenty-third century, the forests of Yellowstone will burn again.

THINK IT OVER

1. What is the major problem in the selection and how is it solved?

2. Besides rainfall, from where else does the Yellowstone area usually get moisture?

3. During which three months does rain normally fall on Yellowstone National Park?

4. Is it usually a good idea to let a fire burn without stopping it? Tell your reasons for thinking as you do.

5. Do you think the story is an example of making the best of a disaster? Tell why you think as you do.

Background and Above:
Fireweed thrives after fires or in disturbed areas, including along roadsides.

WRITE

The park managers changed their policy about fighting all forest fires. Write a persuasive paragraph for a news story, telling why you think that was a wise or an unwise decision.

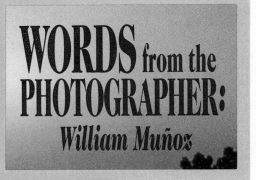

This photograph of William Muñoz feeding a baby camel shows his interest in wildlife.

AWARD-WINNING PHOTOGRAPHER

In the summer of 1988, when the fires started, Dorothy Hinshaw Patent, the author of *Yellowstone Fires: Flames and Rebirth,* began talking to me about doing a book. In September, I went to Yellowstone Park and started taking pictures. The park was closed, but I got a permit to go in and take photographs of the fire damage. When I got the photos back, it was clear that we could return in the spring, and see the rebirth.

I take many, many pictures for a book like this. If there is a particular theme we want to bring out—in this case, it was the damage and the new growth—I try to find pictures that will show that. This was a very hot fire, and we wanted our readers to be able to see the bare, scorched earth that was left behind.

Living in Montana, I know the kind of destruction a forest fire can cause. In fact, I went to Yellowstone expecting to see things worse than they actually were. Radio, television, and newspapers sometimes make things sound worse than they are. What people don't always realize is that there are positive things about forest fires. Yellowstone was very overgrown. It needed to be cleaned out. There are areas that now have new growth in them, new grasses and wildflowers. Those areas will probably become a big meadow, which is very positive. Meadows support more wildlife than forests do.

Down by Lake Yellowstone, in a burn area, I recently saw a new osprey nest. This osprey would not have nested in the forest. Ospreys need an open area. In the next twenty years, if the number of ospreys increases in the park as a result of the fire, that's a positive thing.

PROBLEMS AND SOLUTIONS

You have just read two selections about how the lack of rainfall can cause drought. What kinds of things might have happened in each story if the lack of rainfall had continued longer than it did?

. . . .

Do you think the same method Ki-pat uses to bring rain to Kapiti Plain would have worked at Yellowstone? Give your reasons for thinking the way you do.

. . . .

WRITER'S WORKSHOP   Imagine that you are a newspaper reporter. Work with a partner to report on a flood, a hurricane, or another natural disaster. Choose a disaster and research it. Think about a photograph you have taken at the scene, and write a caption for it. Then write a newspaper article telling about the disaster. Include a drawing of your photograph.

160

BEING CLEVER

How much difference is there between playing a trick and being clever? Careful thinking is needed for each one. As you read the selections that follow, you will see how being clever *and* tricky helps solve some problems but may create others.

C O N T E N T S

Lon Po Po

A RED-RIDING HOOD STORY FROM CHINA

ED YOUNG

Once, long ago, there was a woman who lived alone in the country with her three children, Shang, Tao, and Paotze. On the day of their grandmother's birthday, the good mother set off to see her, leaving the three children at home.

Before she left, she said, "Be good while I am away, my heart-loving children; I will not return tonight. Remember to close the door tight at sunset and latch it well."

But an old wolf lived nearby and saw the good mother leave. At dusk, disguised as an old woman, he came up to the house of the children and knocked on the door twice: bang, bang.

Shang, who was the eldest, said through the latched door, "Who is it?"

"My little jewels," said the wolf, "this is your grandmother, your Po Po."

CALDECOTT MEDAL

ALA NOTABLE BOOK

CHILDREN'S CHOICE

"Po Po!" Shang said. "Our mother has gone to visit you!"

The wolf acted surprised. "To visit me? I have not met her along the way. She must have taken a different route."

"Po Po!" Shang said. "How is it that you come so late?"

The wolf answered, "The journey is long, my children, and the day is short."

Shang listened through the door. "Po Po," she said, "why is your voice so low?"

"Your grandmother has caught a cold, good children, and it is dark and windy out here. Quickly open up, and let your Po Po come in," the cunning wolf said.

Tao and Paotze could not wait. One unlatched the door and the other opened it. They shouted "Po Po, Po Po, come in!"

At the moment he entered the door, the wolf blew out the candle.

"Po Po," Shang asked, "why did you blow out the candle? The room is now dark."

The wolf did not answer.

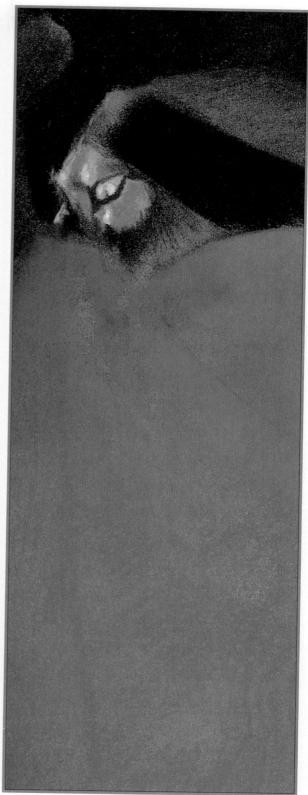

Tao and Paotze rushed to their Po Po and wished to be hugged. The old wolf held Tao. "Good child, you are so plump." He embraced Paotze. "Good child, you have grown to be so sweet."

Soon the old wolf pretended to be sleepy. He yawned. "All the chicks are in the coop," he said. "Po Po is sleepy too." When he climbed into the big bed, Paotze climbed in at one end with the wolf, and Shang and Tao climbed in at the other.

But when Shang stretched, she touched the wolf's tail. "Po Po, Po Po, your foot has a bush on it."

"Po Po has brought hemp strings to weave you a basket," the wolf said.

Shang touched grandmother's sharp claws. "Po Po, Po Po, your hand has thorns on it."

"Po Po has brought an awl to make shoes for you," the wolf said.

At once, Shang lit the light and the wolf blew it out again, but Shang had seen the wolf's hairy face.

"Po Po, Po Po," she said, for she was not only the eldest, she was the most clever, "you must be hungry. Have you eaten gingko nuts?"

"What is gingko?" the wolf asked.

"Gingko is soft and tender, like the skin of a baby. One taste and you will live forever," Shang said, "and the nuts grow on the top of the tree just outside the door."

The wolf gave a sigh. "Oh, dear. Po Po is old, her bones have become brittle. No longer can she climb trees."

"Good Po Po, we can pick some for you," Shang said.

The wolf was delighted.

Shang jumped out of bed and Tao and Paotze came with her to the gingko tree. There, Shang told her sisters about the wolf and all three climbed up the tall tree.

The wolf waited and waited. Plump Tao did not come back. Sweet Paotze did not come back. Shang did not come back, and no one brought any nuts from the gingko tree. At last the wolf shouted, "Where are you, children?"

"Po Po," Shang called out, "we are on the top of the tree eating gingko nuts."

"Good children," the wolf begged, "pluck some for me."

"But Po Po, gingko is magic only when it is plucked directly from the tree. You must come and pluck it from the tree yourself."

The wolf came outside and paced back and forth under the tree where he heard the three children eating the gingko nuts at the top. "Oh, Po Po, these nuts are so tasty! The skin so tender," Shang said. The wolf's mouth began to water for a taste.

Finally, Shang, the eldest and most clever child, said, "Po Po, Po Po, I have a plan. At the door there is a big basket. Behind it is a rope. Tie the rope to the basket, sit in the basket and throw the other end to me. I can pull you up."

The wolf was overjoyed and fetched the basket and the rope, then threw one end of the rope to the top of the tree. Shang caught the rope and began to pull the basket up and up.

Halfway she let go of the rope, and the basket and the wolf fell to the ground.

"I am so small and weak, Po Po," Shang pretended. "I could not hold the rope alone."

"This time I will help," Tao said. "Let us do it again."

The wolf had only one thought in his mind: to taste a gingko nut. He climbed into the basket again. Now Shang and Tao pulled the rope on the basket together, higher and higher.

Again, they let go, and again the wolf tumbled down, down, and bumped his head.

The wolf was furious. He growled. "We could not hold the rope, Po Po," Shang said, "but only one gingko nut and you will be well again."

"I shall give a hand to my sisters this time," Paotze, the youngest, said. "This time we shall not fail."

Now the children pulled the rope with all of their strength. As they pulled they sang, "Hei yo, hei yo," and the basket rose straight up, higher than the first time, higher than the second time, higher and higher and higher until it nearly reached the top of the tree. When the wolf reached out, he could almost touch the highest branch.

But at that moment, Shang coughed and they all let go of the rope, and the basket fell down and down and down. Not only did the wolf bump his head, but he broke his heart to pieces.

"Po Po," Shang shouted, but there was no answer.

"Po Po," Tao shouted, but there was no answer.

"Po Po," Paotze shouted. There was still no answer. The children climbed to the branches just above the wolf and saw that he was truly dead. Then they climbed down, went into the house, closed the door, locked the door with the latch and fell peacefully asleep.

On the next day, their mother returned with baskets of food from their real Po Po, and the three sisters told her the story of the Po Po who had come.

THINK IT OVER

1. How do the girls outsmart the wolf?

2. Even though the lights are out, Shang realizes it is the wolf instead of their Po Po in the house. How does she know?

3. What clues let you know that the wolf was hungry?

4. Why does the wolf pretend to be the girls' Po Po?

WRITE

What are some ways that you can tell if you can trust someone? Make a list.

WORDS ABOUT THE
AUTHOR
AND
ILLUSTRATOR:
ED YOUNG

AWARD-WINNING
AUTHOR AND
ILLUSTRATOR

Ed Young was born in China in 1931, the Chinese Year of the Sheep. There is a belief among the Chinese that people born in the Year of the Sheep are good at art. That belief is true of Ed Young.

Mr. Young grew up in Shanghai, one of China's biggest cities. People from all over the world live in Shanghai. Ed Young had friends from many races and cultures. He liked living with so many different kinds of people.

As a boy, Ed Young had a busy imagination. "I drew everything that happened to cross my mind," he remembers, "airplanes, people, a tall ship that my father was very proud of, a hunter and a bird dog that came out of my head—I have always been happiest doing my own thing."

When Mr. Young was twenty years old, he came to the United States. He soon decided to study art and to work for a magazine. "I knew no matter what I did in life, it would have to be first and foremost related to art," he says. After a few years, he began to illustrate children's books.

Making the illustrations for *Lon Po Po* took some special thinking. To make his drawings look real, Mr. Young had to learn how wolves communicate with their bodies. He also had to remember how the children in China lived and even how the trees grew. Ed Young feels that if he learns everything about the people and the places in a story, his drawings can help make them real to others.

When he is working on a book, Mr. Young starts with a tiny picture, about two inches square. He doesn't plan this picture. "It just comes out of my head," he says. Then he goes to the book editor to talk about ideas for the book. They also decide when the book must be finished. After that, Mr. Young reads about the place where the story happens and makes a set of pictures. "Then I can see what I don't know about the story," he says. He keeps studying until he finds what he needs to know. Finally, he decides on the best kind of pictures to illustrate the story. He may choose to make paper collages, water color paintings, or pencil drawings to match the mood of the story.

Mr. Young thinks the story and pictures need to work together to make a good book. "There are things that words can do that pictures never can," he says. He also thinks there are pictures that words can never describe. The story and pictures together should do what neither one can do alone.

THE CROW
AND
THE PITCHER

from *Belling the Cat and Other Aesop's Fables*

retold in verse by Tom Paxton

"I'm dying of thirst!" cawed the crow in despair.
He looked in a pitcher—some water was there!
He stuck in his beak for a drink, but—hello—
It seemed that the level of water was low.
His beak couldn't reach it,
His chances looked slim,
But then an idea came leaping at him.
He picked up a pebble, flew back in a flash;
It dropped in the pitcher and fell with a splash.
Again and again came the black-feathered flier.
Each pebble that fell brought the sweet water higher.
At last, when the water was near to the brink,
This quick-thinking bird took a well-deserved drink.
So wisdom informs us in this little rhyme,
That little by little will work every time.

AWARD-WINNING
AUTHOR

Cricket and Mountain Lion

AWARD-WINNING
AUTHOR

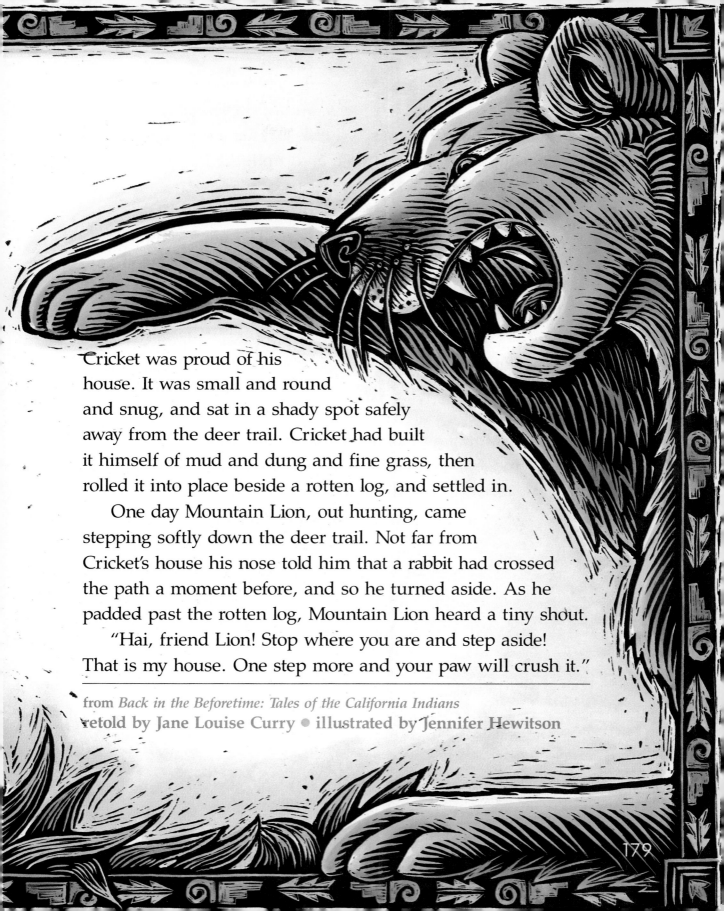

Cricket was proud of his
house. It was small and round
and snug, and sat in a shady spot safely
away from the deer trail. Cricket had built
it himself of mud and dung and fine grass, then
rolled it into place beside a rotten log, and settled in.

One day Mountain Lion, out hunting, came
stepping softly down the deer trail. Not far from
Cricket's house his nose told him that a rabbit had crossed
the path a moment before, and so he turned aside. As he
padded past the rotten log, Mountain Lion heard a tiny shout.

"Hai, friend Lion! Stop where you are and step aside!
That is my house. One step more and your paw will crush it."

from *Back in the Beforetime: Tales of the California Indians*
retold by Jane Louise Curry • illustrated by Jennifer Hewitson

179

Mountain Lion looked around to see who had spoken. When he spied little Cricket atop the log, he laughed. And then he roared until the leaves on the trees trembled.

"Miserable little creature!" he screamed. "Do *you* mean to tell *me* where I may walk? I am Mountain Lion. Not even Eagle can command me. Because I am strong and smart and swift, the forest is mine. And yet you dare to tell me where to step!"

"You may rule the forest, Big Paws," piped Cricket, "but I am Chief in my house and ruler of the land it sits on. So step aside. I do not care to have my house flattened."

Mountain Lion was amazed at Cricket's daring. "Indeed!" roared he. "I will flatten it and you too, if I wish. If I wish, little squeaker, I can crush you and all your folk under my paw."

Cricket gave an angry hop. "Hai, you think so? Take care. I may be small but I have a cousin not half so big as I am who is a great fighter. He can master a Grizzly Bear. So take care!"

"Ho-ho!" Mountain Lion laughed. "I must meet this brave warrior, little boaster. Bring your cousin to this place tomorrow, Cricket, and we will fight. He shall not master *me*. I will flatten him and you and your house together."

And he turned back the way he had come.

The next day at noon Mountain Lion came loping down the deer track and turned aside at the rotten log.

"Hai, small boaster!" he cried. "I am here. Where is your fierce little cousin?"

Cricket did not answer.

"Ho!" roared Mountain Lion. "Come out, brave cousin, and be crushed!"

Soon there came a buzzing by his ear, loud and then louder still. And then a sharp, stabbing sting.

"Oh-ho-yo!" roared Mountain Lion. "Get out of my ear!"

But Mosquito, Cricket's cousin, only sang a louder song and went on stinging.

"Ai-hai-yi!" yowled Mountain Lion.

Cricket sat on his log and watched as Mountain Lion shook his head and leaped and howled. When at last poor Mountain Lion threw himself upon the ground and groaned, Cricket spoke up.

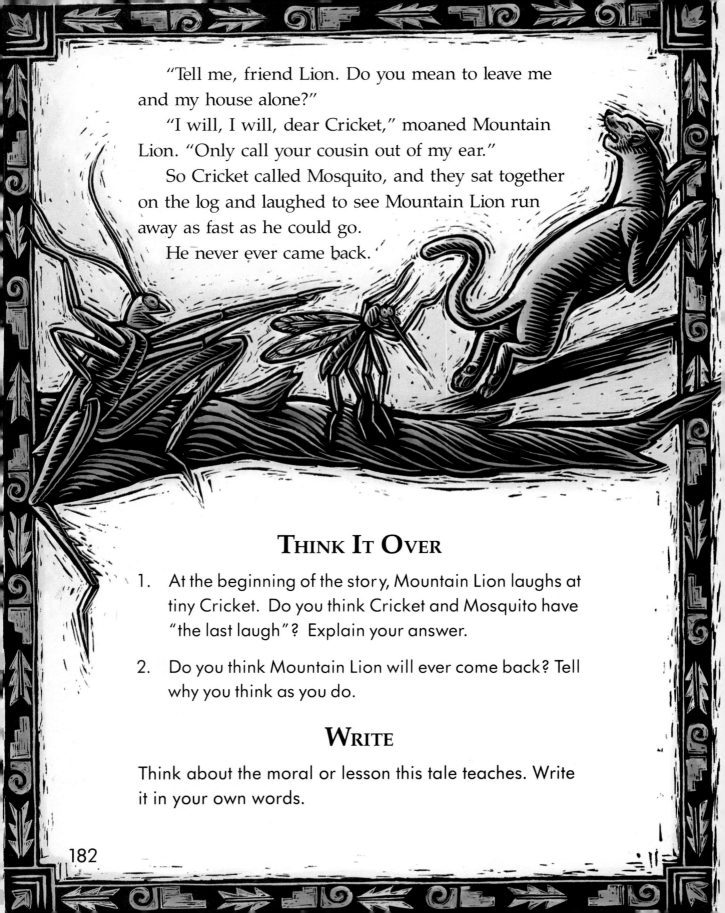

"Tell me, friend Lion. Do you mean to leave me and my house alone?"

"I will, I will, dear Cricket," moaned Mountain Lion. "Only call your cousin out of my ear."

So Cricket called Mosquito, and they sat together on the log and laughed to see Mountain Lion run away as fast as he could go.

He never ever came back.

THINK IT OVER

1. At the beginning of the story, Mountain Lion laughs at tiny Cricket. Do you think Cricket and Mosquito have "the last laugh"? Explain your answer.

2. Do you think Mountain Lion will ever come back? Tell why you think as you do.

WRITE

Think about the moral or lesson this tale teaches. Write it in your own words.

BEING CLEVER

Many of the characters in the stories you have just read are outsmarted by others. Do you think the crow is as clever as Cricket? Explain why you think as you do.

. . . .

Think about a clever character from one of your favorite books, stories, or movies. What character traits or special qualities does that character have in common with the characters in the selections you have just read?

. . . .

WRITER'S WORKSHOP Imagine that you are the size of Cricket. What else could you do to make Mountain Lion pay attention to you? Use one of your ideas to rewrite the story with a different ending.

183

USING YOUR WITS

R iddles, puzzles, and mysteries often have problems that you need to figure out before you can solve them. Some solutions are easy to find. For others, you have to try and try again. See if you can figure out the solutions as you read the mysterious selections that follow.

C O N T E N T S

185

THE PIZZA

AWARD-WINNING
AUTHORS

MONSTER

by Marjorie and Mitchell Sharmat

Who should you call when you're in trouble?

Olivia Sharp. That's me.

My friends call me Olivia.

My enemies call me Liver.

I have a best friend, Taffy Plimpton. But she moved away to Carmel. The next day I went out and got an owl named Hoot. She promised me she wouldn't move away.

Hoot and I live in a penthouse at the top of Pacific Heights with my chauffeur, Willie, my housekeeper, Mrs. Fridgeflake, and my folks.

But my folks aren't home much. This month they're in Paris.

Mrs. Fridgeflake is home all the time. But as far as I'm concerned, she might as well be in Paris. She's always busy flicking specks from glasses, fluffing pillows, and waxing plants.

Our penthouse has twelve bedrooms. I use two of them. One to be myself in and one to be a special agent in.

I have three telephones, one of them red.

I wasn't always a special agent. After Taffy moved away, I used to sit around a lot in my furry white chair and look out my huge living room window at the boats going back and forth on San Francisco Bay.

Fantastic view.

But even when I looked at it with Hoot on my shoulder, I still felt lonely.

I'd never tell anybody that!

It was my secret.

My problem.

One night I said to Hoot, "I bet there must be a trillion secret problems out there. Waiting to be solved."

I'm good at solving problems, except for my own.

I'm good at keeping secrets, too.

I kept talking to Hoot. "If you're good at something, you shouldn't waste it, right?"

Hoot looked at me, silent but wise.

I could tell her answer was a definite YES.

And that's when I, Olivia Sharp, got into the agent business.

The next day I had Willie drive me to a print shop.

I had some ads printed up.

They all said:

DO YOU HAVE A
SECRET PROBLEM?

ARE YOU IN TROUBLE?

DO YOU NEED HELP?

YOU NEED ME.

CALL OLIVIA SHARP
Agent for Secrets
555–4848

Willie and I put up the ads around the city.

On telephone poles.

On street signs.

In store windows.

At the post office.

On school bulletin boards.

Everywhere!

Then I hooked up my special red telephone and I was ready for business.

I was setting up my files when I got my first call.

I answered immediately.

"Olivia Sharp, Agent for Secrets, here," I said.

I heard a sigh.

Then a voice said, "The world is coming to an end."

It was Duncan. I knew him from school.

"The world is coming to an end," he said again.

"That's what you always say." I strung three paper clips together. Why was he bothering me!

"I saw your ad at the pizza store," he said. "Can you help me?"

"I can't stop the world from coming to an end," I told him. "I'm good, but not that good."

"You don't understand," Duncan said. "I lost my best friend. Don't tell anybody."

"I'm good at keeping secrets," I said. "Stay put. I'll be right over."

I slammed down the receiver and rang for Willie to bring the limo around.

Then I went to the closet and got my boa.

When I hit the street, Willie was waiting with the limo. "Where to, Miss Olivia?" he asked.

"To Duncan's, and hurry. It's an emergency."

"You've got it, Boss," said Willie as we rolled out of the courtyard and through the big iron gates leading onto Steiner Street.

While we rode up and down the hills to Duncan's flat,
I remembered something. Duncan didn't *have* any friends.
So how could he lose his best one? Duncan is *so*
depressing. He's always saying that the world is coming
to an end. And nobody likes to hear that. I know I don't,
but a client is a client.

When we got to Duncan's, I told Willie to wait. I
should have told him to give me a piggyback ride. Duncan
lives in a flat on the fourth floor of a walk-up.

I was out of breath when I knocked on
Duncan's door.

He answered it.

Duncan's hair was hanging over his
eyes as if half his face was hiding
from the world. His socks drooped
over his sneakers, and his baggy
blue jeans were slipping over his hips.

All of Duncan seemed to be on
the way down. This guy was a real
downer all right!

"Where did you lose this best
friend of yours, and who is he?"
I asked Duncan.

"It's Desiree, and I lost her
inside Angelo's Pizza Parlor,"
he said.

"That's only around the corner," I said. "How could you lose her there?"

"We went into Angelo's to get pizza. I ordered a slice for her and a slice for me. When the slices came, I handed Desiree one of them. And that's when I lost her."

"You gave Desiree a slice of pizza and she disappeared? Did she go in a puff of garlic or something?"

I laughed and fluffed my boa.

Duncan never laughs. What with the world coming to an end and all that rot.

He said, "Desiree didn't even eat her slice. She got mad and left the pizza parlor. That's how I lost my best friend."

Duncan pulled something out of his pocket.

"I saved her slice. Want it?"

Duncan dangled a limp little piece of cold pizza right under my nose.

I stepped backward.

Then I looked down at the pizza.

"This slice is very small," I said. "Was the one you kept for yourself bigger?"

Duncan shrugged. "I didn't measure them. I ate mine up and then I went home and called Desiree. But she hung up on me."

"Maybe you can get another friend. On second thought, that's not likely. I've got it. Get another pizza—a whole one—and give it to Desiree."

Duncan's face dropped. It was always doing that. "I'm out of money. I spent my last cent at Angelo's."

"Never fear, Olivia's here." I opened my purse and peeled off a ten-dollar bill. "This should cover it. Go back to Angelo's immediately and order a pizza to go. A large pizza with everything on it. Tie a huge red ribbon around the box. Take it to Desiree's house and give it to her. I'm glad I could help."

I went back downstairs to Willie and the limo. It was a lot easier walking down than climbing up.

I always feel I deserve a small reward when I've helped someone. I had Willie take us to the Bon Ton Chocolate Shop for two of their superdooper ice-cream sodas.

When I got home, my red phone was ringing.

It was Duncan.

"How did it go?" I asked.

"Disasterville," he said. "Desiree said the ribbon was pretty. While she was untying it, I told her what was inside the box. Then suddenly she gave me a weird look and shoved the box back at me."

I had had the ice-cream soda too soon.

Duncan was still talking. "The box split open. The pizza slid out. Now I still have no best friend and I'm smeared from head to toe with tomato sauce, cheese, mushrooms, and anchovies. I look like a gooey pizza monster!"

I could almost see Duncan dripping pizza stuff. When I started in this agent business, I never expected to have a

pizza monster for my first client. But I stayed cool. "I'll think of something else," I said. "You can depend upon Olivia Sharp."

"Hurry! The world is coming to an end," Duncan said, and he hung up.

I went to the window and looked out at the bay. A garbage barge was going by.

I knew what had gone wrong. How could I expect just one pizza, even with everything on it, to solve Duncan's problem?

I looked up Desiree's address.

I rang for Willie.

"Willie," I said, "find the name of a pizza bakery, and order fifty different kinds of pizzas to be sent to Desiree. Enclose a card saying *I hope you like one of these. From your best friend, Duncan.*"

"You've got it, Boss," Willie said.

That should take care of that, I thought. It's nice to be really, really rich and able to help others.

I stuck my feet up in the air.

I painted my toenails and wiggled them dry.

I fed Hoot.

Sometimes she hoots.

Sometimes she doesn't.

Sometimes I'm as wise as she is.

Sometimes I'm not.

I was in the bathtub when the red telephone rang.

I grabbed my robe, rushed to my office, answered my phone, and heard, "The world has now come to an end."

It was Duncan, of course.

"Tell me about it," I said.

"Desiree just called me. She's madder than ever. She said she doesn't want fifty pizzas. What does she mean?"

"No problem," I said to him. "I'll look into it."

I hung up.

I had a real problem, but I never admit that to a client. Desiree had turned down a slice of pizza, a whole pizza, and now fifty pizzas. And she was very mad. There had to be more to this than a too-small slice of pizza!

I got dressed and rang for Willie to bring the limo around.

"To Desiree's place," I said.

When we got to Desiree's apartment house, we couldn't find a place to park, so I told Willie to circle the block.

Five circles later, I was out of the car and heading toward Desiree's front door. She lives on the ground floor.

The fifty pizzas were blocking the way.

I picked my way through them.

I pounded on Desiree's door.

She opened it.

Desiree turned out to be one of those perfect scrub-a-dub-dub blondes who ties her hair back in a ponytail with a rainbow-colored ribbon. Without looking down I knew she'd be wearing shiny patent-leather, pointy-toed shoes that she could tippy-tap across the room in. I could see why Duncan liked her. Myself, I can't stand the type.

"I'm here about Duncan," I said, handing her my card.

Olivia Sharp
AGENT FOR SECRETS
I CAN FIX ANYTHING.
555-4848

I stuck my foot inside her door while I spoke. I wasn't going to take any chance she'd slam the door in my face when she heard why I was there. That's a trick we agents have.

"Come in," Desiree said without noticing that I was already partway in.

I flung my boa on the sofa in her living room.

I said, "Duncan hired me to find his lost best friend. You. Don't you know it's wrong to get angry about a slice of pizza?"

I knew that wasn't why Desiree was mad at Duncan. I was fishing. Secret agents have to do that.

"The pizza was just an excuse," Desiree said. "I don't want to be Duncan's friend. He's so . . . so . . ."

"Depressing?" I offered. "Totally, totally depressing?"

"Right," Desiree said. "He's no fun at all."

"So why did you go into Angelo's Pizza Parlor with him?"

"He came along just as I was going inside. He said, 'Getting a piece of pizza? Me too.' So we went in together. When our slices came, he handed me one."

"And?"

"He said, 'Have a piece of this gucky, yucky, slimy pizza, which has dead cheese and dying mushrooms on it.' That's why I left. Do you blame me?"

Desiree didn't expect an answer. She folded my boa neatly and went on talking.

"Later on, Duncan brought a whole pizza to my house in a box tied with a pretty red ribbon. While I was untying the ribbon he said, 'Here's the slimiest pizza with all the guckiest, yuckiest things in the world on it. It probably died on the way over.'"

"That sounds like Duncan," I said.

"Yes," Desiree said. "He can even make Angelo's pizza look disgusting. Who needs a friend like that?"

Nobody, I thought. That was the whole trouble. Nobody.

I took a hard look at Desiree. She was tugging at her ribbon. Her rainbow was unraveling. Duncan can do that to you. Unravel rainbows and all of that.

But he was my client.

I knew what I had to do.

I grabbed my boa. "I must dash off," I said.

I left.

At the front door, the neighborhood dogs and cats were gathering around the pizzas.

"Feast!" I called as I got into my limo.

"To the main library," I said to Willie.

The library has absolutely tons and tons of books. Willie whisked me there.

I checked out ten jokebooks.

"To Duncan's," I said to Willie.

When we got to Duncan's building, Willie helped me carry the ten books up to the fourth floor.

Duncan opened the door on the first knock.

We handed him the books.

"Here. Read these!" I gasped while I tried to catch my breath.

Then Willie and I took off.

When I got home, my red telephone was ringing.

I rushed to answer it.

But I was too late. No one was there.

I flung myself on the couch in my office. This was an exhausting case.

The red telephone rang again.

Duncan was on the line.

"Where have you been?" he asked. "I've been calling and calling. Why did you bring me these dopey jokebooks?"

"To put a smile on your face."

"A smile?" he asked.

"Yes, a smile. That nice curvy thing under the nose that most kids have when they think cheery thoughts. Which, by the way, you never do."

"But you're supposed to help me with Desiree."

"Duncan, darling, Desiree's mad at you because you said awful things about the pizza. You say awful things all the time about *everything*. That's why Desiree doesn't want to be your friend."

"Are you sure?"

"Positive. Listen to me, Duncan. You just said the books I gave you are dopey. Have you even *read* them?"

"No."

"See what I mean? Now I've got something important for you to do, Duncan. Go to your window, look out, and tell me if you can see the world coming to an end."

"Hold on," Duncan said.

He put the receiver down.

I waited.

I tapped my fingers on my desk.

It was taking Duncan forever.

How big a job could it be?

At last he came back to the phone.

"I looked north and I looked south," he said, "but I didn't actually *see* the world coming to an end. I couldn't see east or west because there are buildings in the way."

"Believe me," I said, "east and west are in good shape. I checked on them. Okay?"

"Okay," Duncan said. "So the world isn't coming to an end. But what do I do about Desiree?"

"Think happy. Read the jokebooks I gave you. Find a joke you really, really adore. Then call up Desiree and tell it to her fast before she can hang up on you. Then call me back."

I slammed down the receiver.

I waited for Duncan to call back.

I read my horoscope.

I arranged my credit cards in alphabetical order.

I smoothed Hoot's feathers.

The red telephone rang.

Duncan was on the line, laughing.

Laughing!

"I found five great jokes," he said. "Desiree listened to all of them, and she laughed."

"Super," I said.

"She says she's thinking about being my friend."

"Now you're getting somewhere," I said. "All you have to do is keep it up. You don't need me anymore."

"You know Desiree was never my best friend," Duncan said.

"I know it."

"*You* are!" he said.

"Not yet," I said.

I put down the receiver.

I made some notes for my files.

I closed my files and turned out the light in my office.

I went into my other bedroom to be myself.

Tomorrow I'm going to school.

Sometimes I'm a regular kid.

Sometimes I'm not.

HELPED DUNCAN.

BE SURE TO FOLLOW UP.

RETURN LIBRARY BOOKS WITHIN 2 WEEKS.

MET A NEW GIRL, DESIREE.
SHE'S PERFECT, NEEDS HELP BADLY.

★★★ MESSAGE TO MYSELF: ★★★
SOMETIMES MONEY CAN SOLVE PROBLEMS.
BUT SOMETIMES IT CAN'T.

THINK IT OVER

1. Describe the case Olivia was working on and how she solved it.

2. How did Olivia know that Desiree was not Duncan's best friend?

3. How did Olivia prove the statements "Sometimes money can solve problems. But sometimes it can't"?

4. Do you think Olivia is a good secret agent? Tell why you think as you do.

WRITE

Would you ask Olivia to help you solve a problem? Make a list of reasons why you would or would not go to Olivia for help.

Have you ever wondered what your family tree looks like? I mean, the real lowdown on your parents? What your great-grandparents were like? That kind of thing. Well, I did, and since I'm sort of a detective, I decided to do a deep background check on where I came from.

It didn't take me long. I went to the library and looked up my name. There I was in big letters: OLIVIA SHARP.

I was born in 1987 in Tucson, Arizona. The brain-child of Mitchell and Marjorie Sharmat. They have many other children. Two of them are real, and hundreds of them are fictional, just like me. Maybe you know Mitchell's Gregory, the Terrible Eater, or Marjorie's Nate the Great?

The Sharmats tried hard to pick the right name for me. First, Mitchell thought of Gertrude Gumshoe (awful, huh?). Then there were Jennifer, Danielle, Tiffany, Nicole, Stephanie, and plenty of others, including Bianca Bunko (*really* awful!). Finally . . . Olivia Sharp, and they knew it was the real me.

The Sharmats decided that I should live in San Francisco, in a penthouse, and that I should travel around in a limo. The Sharmats went to San Francisco, hired a limo, scouted the neighborhood where they thought I should live and go to school. They even found a pizza parlor for *The Pizza Monster.*

AWARD-WINNING
AUTHORS

204

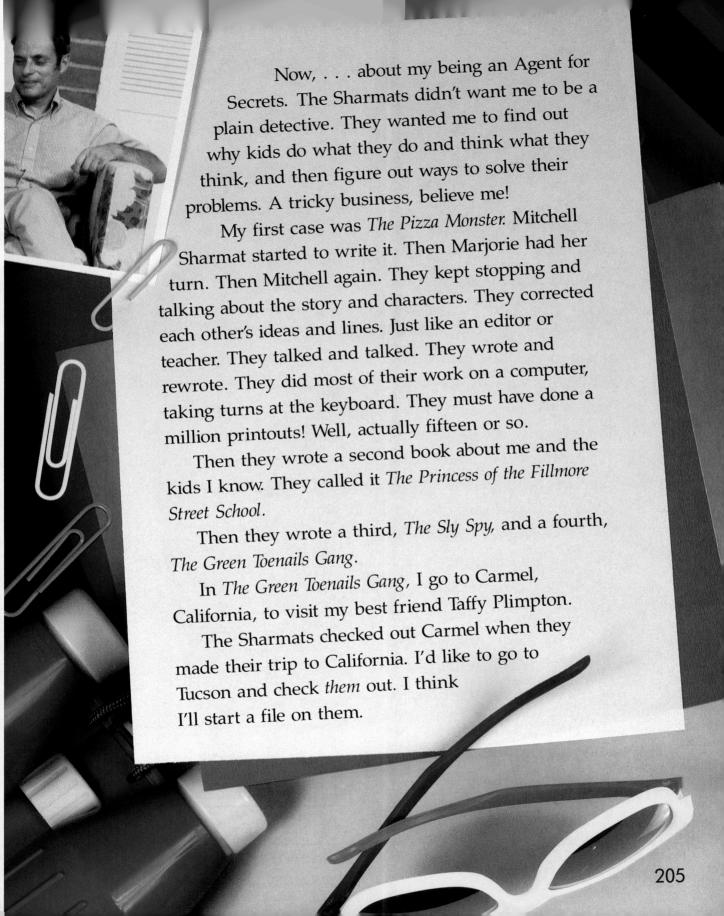

Now, . . . about my being an Agent for Secrets. The Sharmats didn't want me to be a plain detective. They wanted me to find out why kids do what they do and think what they think, and then figure out ways to solve their problems. A tricky business, believe me!

My first case was *The Pizza Monster*. Mitchell Sharmat started to write it. Then Marjorie had her turn. Then Mitchell again. They kept stopping and talking about the story and characters. They corrected each other's ideas and lines. Just like an editor or teacher. They talked and talked. They wrote and rewrote. They did most of their work on a computer, taking turns at the keyboard. They must have done a million printouts! Well, actually fifteen or so.

Then they wrote a second book about me and the kids I know. They called it *The Princess of the Fillmore Street School*.

Then they wrote a third, *The Sly Spy*, and a fourth, *The Green Toenails Gang*.

In *The Green Toenails Gang*, I go to Carmel, California, to visit my best friend Taffy Plimpton. The Sharmats checked out Carmel when they made their trip to California. I'd like to go to Tucson and check *them* out. I think I'll start a file on them.

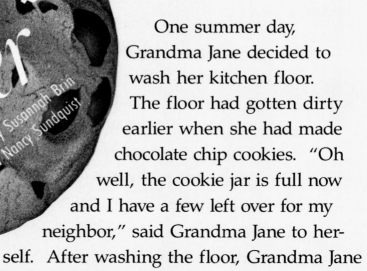

CHOCOLATE CHIP COOKIE Caper

by Susannah Brin and Nancy Sundquist

One summer day, Grandma Jane decided to wash her kitchen floor. The floor had gotten dirty earlier when she had made chocolate chip cookies. "Oh well, the cookie jar is full now and I have a few left over for my neighbor," said Grandma Jane to herself. After washing the floor, Grandma Jane decided to take her neighbor the plate of extra cookies while the floor dried. She closed the kitchen window and locked the back door. On the way to the neighbor's, she passed Tony the gardener. Tony was planting seeds in the flower bed. Then she passed three-year-old Buddy Sullivan playing in his plastic swimming pool. Grandma Jane gave both Tony and Buddy a chocolate chip cookie.

Later when Grandma Jane returned home, she found that someone had been in her kitchen. Look at the picture below of Grandma Jane's kitchen. The clues in the story and the clues in the picture will help you solve the mystery. Answer the following questions:

❶ How did the thief enter the kitchen?

❷ What did the thief steal?

❸ Who was the thief?

❹ How do you know who the thief was?

illustration by Neal Yamamoto

USING YOUR WITS

Olivia thinks Desiree is perfect yet needs help badly. Why does Olivia think that way? How is Olivia different from Desiree?

. . . .

Think about the mysterious events in "The Pizza Monster" and in "Chocolate Chip Cookie Caper." What clues did the authors give to help you solve the mysteries?

. . . .

WRITER'S WORKSHOP Think about how you would have tried to solve the pizza mystery. What would you have done differently? Imagine that you are applying for a job as a secret agent. Write a persuasive paragraph about yourself. Be sure to list your problem-solving skills and the reasons you should be hired for a job. Then have a classmate interview you for the job. Try to persuade the interviewer to hire you.

CONNECTIONS

Palenque, Mexico

MAYAN MYSTERY

What caused the disappearance of people from the Mayan cities? This is one of the great puzzles of all time. More than a thousand years ago, the Maya built large stone cities in Mexico and Central America. They developed a written language and advanced skills in math. Then, several hundred years later, they suddenly left their cities to be taken over by the jungle.

What happened? Experts once believed that wars or natural disasters caused the people to leave. Now, many people think there may have been food shortages and revolts by the people against their rulers. Still, we may never know the whole truth.

■ In a small group, prepare a report on an ancient Mayan city. Present your report to your classmates, using pictures or models if possible.

CALENDAR SYMBOLS

The Maya developed a calendar of eighteen months, plus an extra five-day period, shown in symbols. Create your own symbols for our twelve-month calendar. Share them with your classmates, and explain your designs.

Tikal Calendar

LOST CITIES

With a partner or small group, find out about another culture's "lost" city, such as Machu Picchu in Peru or Angkor in Kampuchea. List your findings on a chart like the following, and give a short report to your classmates.

MACHU PICCHU

When?	probably built in the 1400s, lasting into the 1500s
Where?	
Description	
What Happened?	

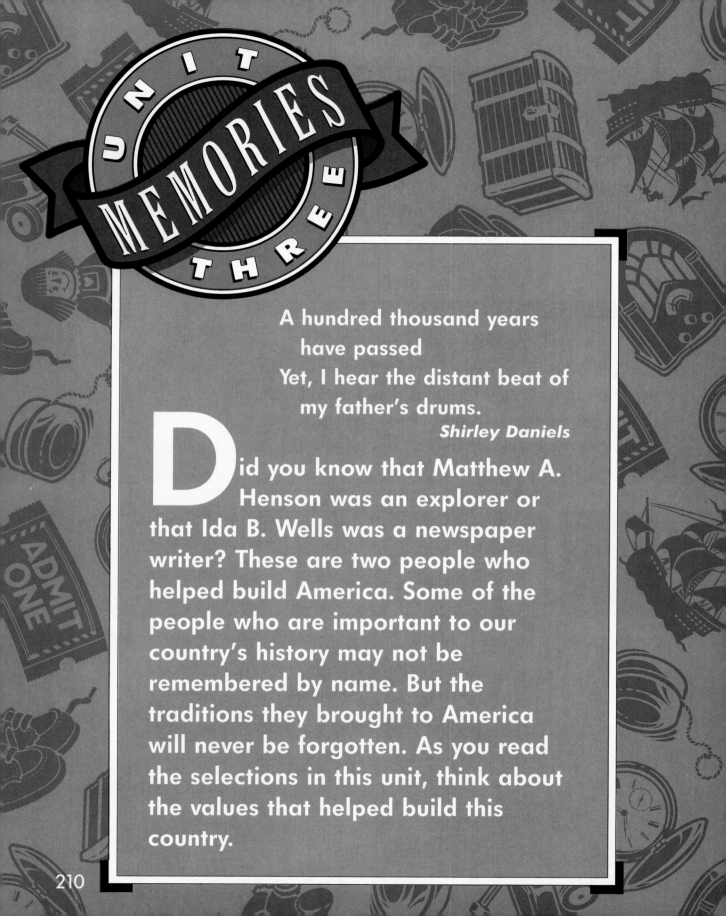

UNIT MEMORIES THREE

A hundred thousand years
have passed
Yet, I hear the distant beat of
my father's drums.

Shirley Daniels

Did you know that Matthew A. Henson was an explorer or that Ida B. Wells was a newspaper writer? These are two people who helped build America. Some of the people who are important to our country's history may not be remembered by name. But the traditions they brought to America will never be forgotten. As you read the selections in this unit, think about the values that helped build this country.

THEMES

REMEMBERING

LOOKING BACK

WAS IT REAL?

BOOKSHELF

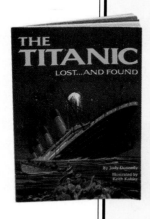

THE TITANIC: LOST . . . AND FOUND
by Judy Donnelly

The ship that was believed to be the safest ship afloat sank on its first voyage. This exciting adventure also tells about how the remains of the famous steamship were discovered many years later.

HBJ LIBRARY BOOK

IN COAL COUNTRY
written by Judith Hendershot
illustrated by Thomas B. Allen

This beautifully illustrated book tells about the excitement and hard work that go along with growing up in a coal-mining community. ALA NOTABLE BOOK, *BOSTON GLOBE–HORN BOOK* HONOR, *NEW YORK TIMES* BEST ILLUSTRATED BOOKS OF THE YEAR

212

ARAMINTA'S PAINT BOX

by Karen Ackerman

Araminta's family is moving to California. Her paint box travels across the country as well, but the two of them have very different adventures.

FROM PATH TO HIGHWAY:
THE STORY OF
THE BOSTON POST ROAD

by Gail Gibbons

Five hundred years ago, Indians followed a narrow path. Today the path is a road connecting New York City and Boston, Massachusetts.   AWARD-WINNING AUTHOR

THE HOUSE ON MAPLE STREET

by Bonnie Pryor

Three hundred years pass before your eyes. In this story you see how the past is still with us today.

AWARD-WINNING AUTHOR

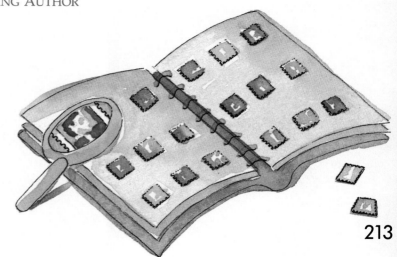

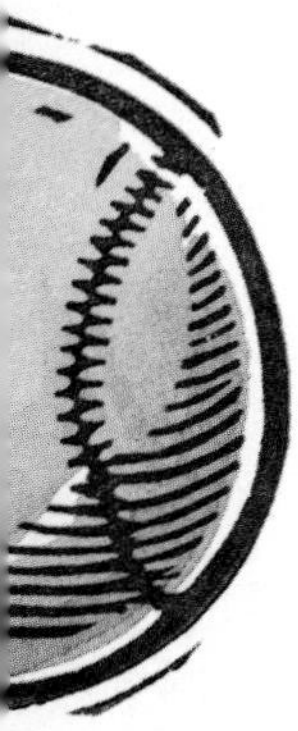

REMEMBERING

Some families save objects they like or follow customs they enjoy and then pass them along to other family members. These objects and traditions are often handed down from one family to the next. The following selections and poems contain examples of the ways traditions are remembered in different people's lives.

C O N T E N T S

When my Great-Gramma Anna came to America, she wore the same thick overcoat and big boots she had worn for farm work. But her family weren't dirt farmers anymore. In New York City her father's work was hauling things on a wagon, and the rest of the family made artificial flowers all day.

TEACHERS'
CHOICE

The Keeping Quilt

Patricia Polacco

Everyone was in a hurry, and it was so crowded, not like in backhome Russia. But all the same it was their home, and most of their neighbors were just like them.

When Anna went to school, English sounded to her like pebbles dropping into shallow water. *Shhhhhh. . . . Shhhhhh. . . . Shhhhhh.* In six months she was speaking English. Her parents almost never learned, so she spoke English for them, too.

218

The only things she had left of backhome Russia were her dress and the babushka she liked to throw up into the air when she was dancing.

And her dress was getting too small. After her mother had sewn her a new one, she took her old dress and babushka. Then from a basket of old clothes she took Uncle Vladimir's shirt, Aunt Havalah's nightdress, and an apron of Aunt Natasha's.

"We will make a quilt to help us always remember home," Anna's mother said. "It will be like having the family in backhome Russia dance around us at night."

And so it was. Anna's mother invited all the neighborhood ladies. They cut out animals and flowers from the scraps of clothing. Anna kept the needles threaded and handed them to the ladies as

they needed them. The border of the quilt was made of Anna's babushka.

On Friday nights Anna's mother would say the prayers that started the Sabbath. The family ate challah[1] and chicken soup. The quilt was the tablecloth.

---

[1]challah [khä′lə]: a loaf of bread often braided before baking

Anna grew up and fell in love with Great-Grandpa
Sasha. To show he wanted to be her husband, he
gave Anna a gold coin, a dried flower, and a piece of
rock salt, all tied into a linen handkerchief. The gold
was for wealth, the flower for love, and the salt so
their lives would have flavor.

She accepted the hankie. They were engaged.

Under the wedding huppa,[2] Anna and Sasha promised each other love and understanding. After the wedding, the men and women celebrated separately.

___

[2]huppa [hōōp′ə]: a canopy under which the Jewish marriage ceremony is performed

When my Grandma Carle was born, Anna wrapped her daughter in the quilt to welcome her warmly into the world. Carle was given a gift of gold, flower, salt, and bread. Gold so she would never know poverty, a flower so she would always know love, salt so her life would always have flavor, and bread so that she would never know hunger.

Carle learned to keep the Sabbath and to cook and clean and do washing.

"Married you'll be someday," Anna told Carle, and . . . again the quilt became a wedding huppa, this time for Carle's wedding to Grandpa George. Men and women celebrated together, but they still did not dance together. In Carle's wedding bouquet was a gold coin, bread, and salt.

Carle and George moved to a farm in Michigan and Great-Gramma Anna came to live with them. The quilt once again wrapped a new little girl, Mary Ellen.

Mary Ellen called Anna, Lady Gramma. She had grown very old and was sick a lot of the time. The quilt kept her legs warm.

On Anna's ninety-eighth birthday, the cake was a kulich[3], a rich cake with raisins and candied fruit in it.

When Great-Gramma Anna died, prayers were said to lift her soul to heaven. My mother Mary Ellen was now grown up.

When Mary Ellen left home, she took the quilt with her.

---

[3]kulich [kōō′lich]: a sweetened, dome-shaped yeast bread or cake

When she became a bride, the quilt became her huppa. For the first time, friends who were not Jews came to the wedding. My mother wore a suit, but in her bouquet were gold, bread, and salt.

The quilt welcomed me, Patricia, into the world . . . and it was the tablecloth for my first birthday party.

At night I would trace my fingers around the edges of each animal on the quilt before I went to sleep. I told my mother stories about the animals on the quilt. She told me whose sleeve had made the horse, whose apron had made the chicken, whose dress had made the flowers, and whose babushka went around the edge of the quilt.

The quilt was a pretend cape when I was in the bullring, or sometimes a tent in the steaming Amazon jungle.

At my wedding to Enzo-Mario, men and women danced together. In my bouquet were gold, bread, and salt.

Twenty years ago I held Traci Denise in the quilt for the first time. Someday she, too, will leave home and she will take the quilt with her.

THINK IT OVER

1. What were all of the uses for the quilt?

2. Where did Great-Gramma Anna live before she came to America?

3. At what point did you find out who was telling the story?

4. What do you think the expression "so their lives would have flavor" means?

WRITE

Think about some traditions that your family passes down or that families you know pass down. Choose one tradition and write a paragraph describing how the tradition began and how it could be passed on to other family members.

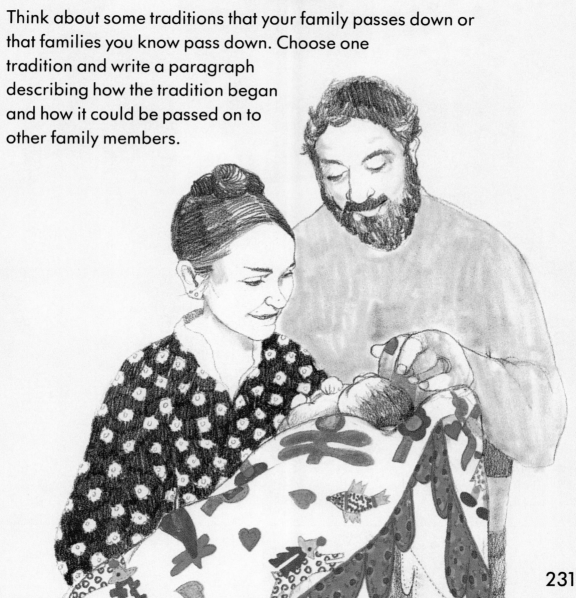

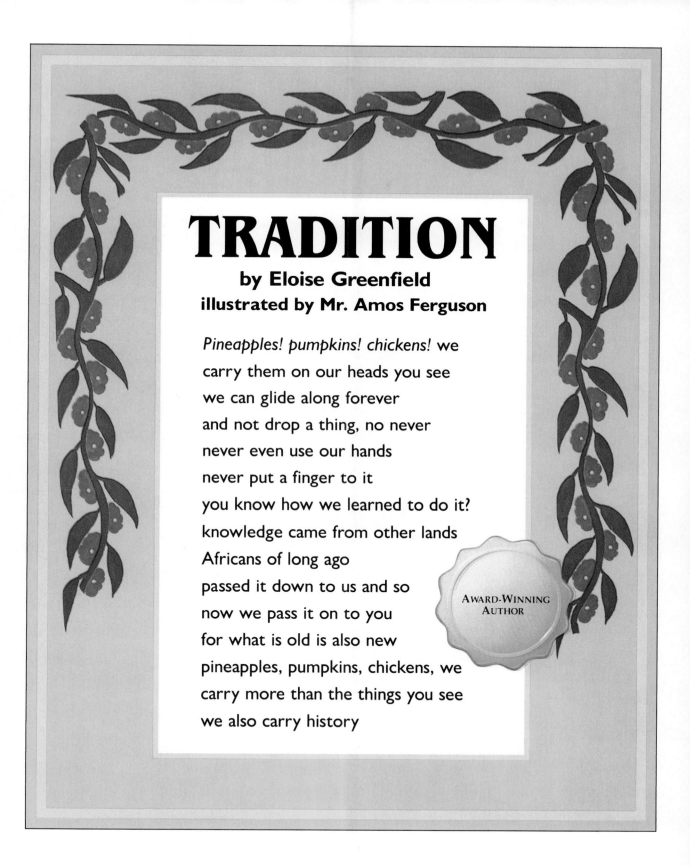

TRADITION

by Eloise Greenfield
illustrated by Mr. Amos Ferguson

Pineapples! pumpkins! chickens! we
carry them on our heads you see
we can glide along forever
and not drop a thing, no never
never even use our hands
never put a finger to it
you know how we learned to do it?
knowledge came from other lands
Africans of long ago
passed it down to us and so
now we pass it on to you
for what is old is also new
pineapples, pumpkins, chickens, we
carry more than the things you see
we also carry history

AWARD-WINNING
AUTHOR

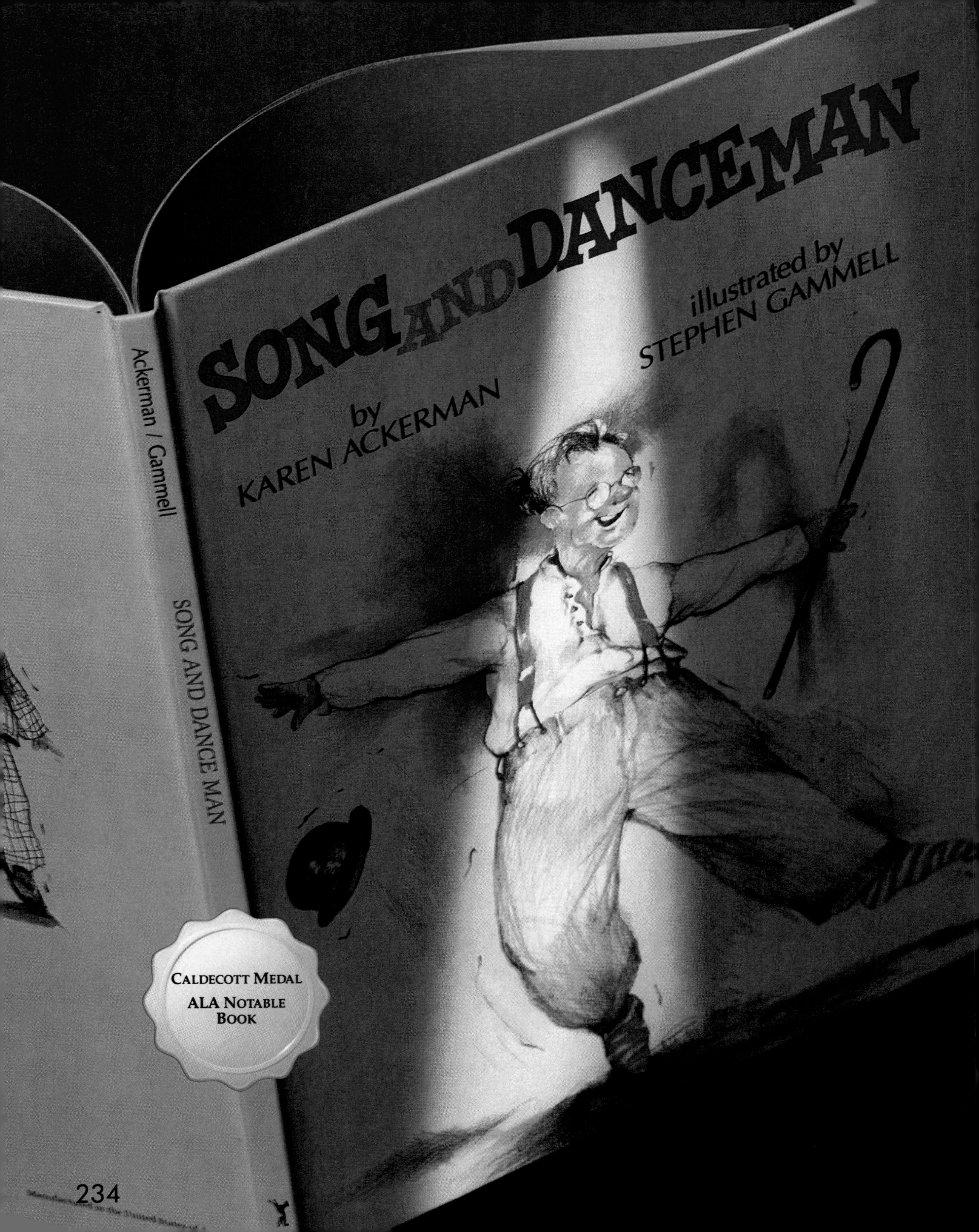

SONG AND DANCE MAN
by
KAREN ACKERMAN
illustrated by
STEPHEN GAMMELL
Ackerman / Gammell
SONG AND DANCE MAN
CALDECOTT MEDAL
ALA NOTABLE BOOK

Grandpa was a song and dance man who once danced on the vaudeville stage.

When we visit, he tells us about a time before people watched TV, back in the good old days, the song and dance days.

"Supper in an hour!" Grandma calls from the kitchen.

"I wonder if my tap shoes still fit?" Grandpa says with a smile. Then he turns on the light to the attic, and we follow him up the steep, wooden steps.

Faded posters of Grandpa when he was young hang on the walls. He moves some cardboard boxes and a rack of Grandma's winter dresses out of the way, and we see a dusty brown, leather-trimmed trunk in the corner.

As soon as Grandpa opens it, the smell of cedar chips and old things saved fills the attic. Inside are his shoes with the silver half-moon taps on the toes and heels, bowler hats and top hats, and vests with stripes and matching bow ties.

We try on the hats and pretend we're dancing on a vaudeville stage, where the bright lights twinkle and the piano player nods his head along with the music.

After wiping his shoes with a cloth he calls a shammy, Grandpa puts them on. He tucks small, white pads inside the shoes so his corns won't rub, and he turns on the lamps and aims each one down like a spotlight.

He sprinkles a little powder on the floor, and it's show time. We sit on one of Grandma's woolen blankets, clap our hands, and call out, "Yay, Grandpa!"

The song and dance man begins to dance the old soft shoe. His feet move slowly at first, while his tap shoes make soft, slippery sounds like rain on a tin roof.

We forget that it's Grandpa dancing, and all we can hear is the silvery tap of two feet, and all we can see is a song and dance man gliding across a vaudeville stage.

He says, "Watch this!" and does a new step that sounds like a woodpecker tapping on a tree. Suddenly, his shoes move faster, and he begins to sing. His voice is as round and strong as a canyon echo, and his cheeks get rosy as he sings "Yankee Doodle Boy," a song he knows from the good old days.

There are too many dance steps and too many words in the song for us to remember, but the show is better than any show on TV.

The song and dance man stops and leans forward with a wink.

"What's that in your ear?" he asks, and he pulls a
silver dollar out of somebody's hair.

He rolls his bowler hat down his arm, catches it in his
hand, and flips it back up onto his head.

"Know how to make an elephant float?" he asks. "One
scoop of ice cream, two squirts of soda, and three scoops
of elephant!"

We've heard that joke before, but the song and dance
man slaps his knees and laughs until his eyes water.

240

He tries to wipe them with a red hanky from his vest pocket, but the hanky just gets longer and longer as he pulls it out. He looks so surprised that we start laughing too, and it feels like the whole attic is shaking.

Sometimes we laugh so hard, the hiccups start, and Grandpa stops to bring us a glass of water from the bathroom.

"Drink slow and hold your breath," he says, "or I'll have to scare you!"

241

Once our hiccups are gone, he gets a gold-tipped cane and a black silk top hat from the trunk. He lowers his eyes and tips the hat, and he's standing very still.

All the lights are turned low except one that shines on his polished tap shoes. It's the grand finale, so the song and dance man takes a deep breath. He lifts the cane and holds it in both hands.

Slowly, he starts to tap. His shoes move faster and faster, and the sounds coming from them are too many to make with only two feet.

He spins and jumps into the air. Touching the stage again, he kneels with his arms spread out, and the silk top hat and gold-tipped cane lie side by side at his feet. His shoes are still, and the show is over.

We stand up together and clap our hands, shouting "Hurray!"
and "More!" but Grandpa only smiles and shakes his head,
all out of breath. He takes off his tap shoes, wraps them
gently in the shammy cloth, and puts them back in the leather-
trimmed trunk. He carefully folds his vest and lays the top hat
and cane on it, and we follow him to the stairway.

Grandpa holds on to the rail as we go down the steps.

At the bottom he hugs us, and we tell him we wish we
could have seen him dance in the good old days, the song and
dance days. He smiles, and whispers that he wouldn't trade a
million good old days for the days he spends with us.

But as he turns off the attic light, Grandpa glances back up
the stairs, and we wonder how much he really misses that time
on the vaudeville stage, when he was a song and dance man.

THINK IT OVER

1. Why do you think Grandpa is called a song and dance man?

2. Where did Grandpa keep the clothes he wore during his song and dance days?

3. Why do you think Grandpa wondered if his tap shoes still fit?

4. How is the kind of show Grandpa put on different from what you might see on television today?

WRITE

Pretend you work for a newspaper. Write a short review telling all about Grandpa's vaudeville act. Remember to describe the costumes, lighting, sound effects, and how the audience responded.

DRUMS Of My FATHER

by Shirley Daniels △ illustrated by Robert Hunt

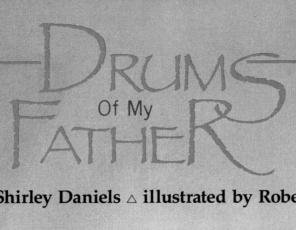

A hundred thousand years have passed
Yet, I hear the distant beat of my father's drums.
I hear his drums throughout the land,
His beat I feel within my heart.

The drums shall beat, so my heart shall beat,
And I shall live a hundred thousand years.

REMEMBERING

In each of the selections you have just read, memories are saved. Explain how each special memory is saved.

. . . .

Reread the poems. Choose one and retell it in your own words. Try to keep the same feeling of remembering in your retelling.

. . . .

WRITER'S WORKSHOP Sometimes friends and relatives can't visit each other very often. When they do visit, something special usually happens. Write a personal narrative that tells about a special time you shared with a friend or relative that you don't see all the time. Then read your narrative to a group of classmates.

247

LOOKING BACK

Sometimes the past holds hidden treasures that have been forgotten over the years. It takes special skills to uncover some of the lost treasures of the past. The selection, the words from the author and illustrator, and the puzzle that follow show how some people can unlock and relive the past while living in the present.

CONTENTS

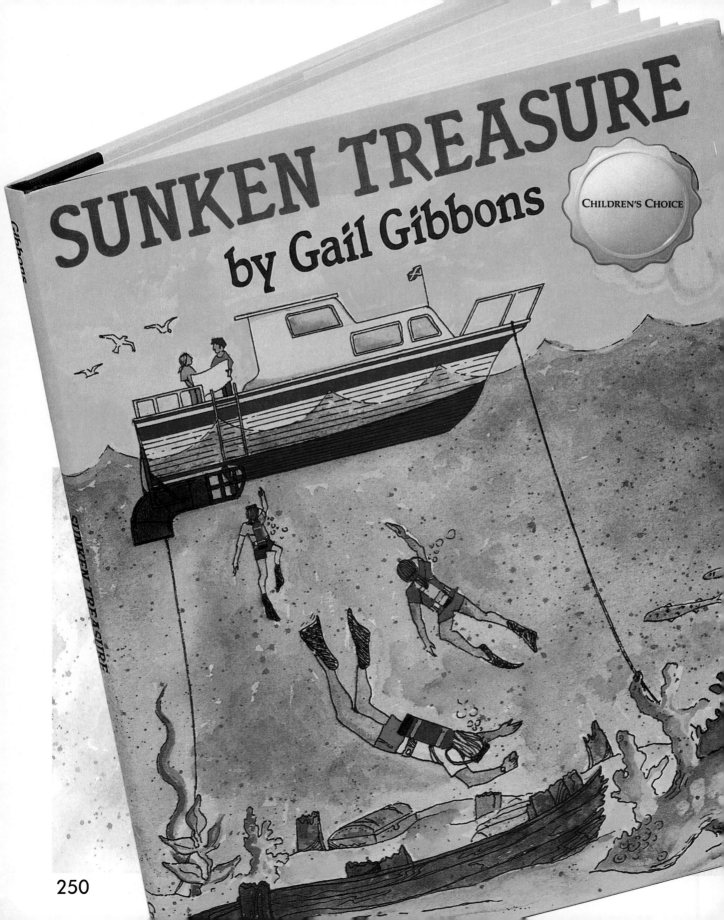

SUNKEN TREASURE
by Gail Gibbons

CHILDREN'S CHOICE

"It's there! It's really there!"

The rotting hull of a ship has been found on the ocean floor. Within the wreck lies a fabulous treasure. The story of each underwater treasure hunt is different, but each goes back to the same beginning . . . the sinking of a ship. The story of the hunt for the *Nuestra Señora de Atocha,* a Spanish galleon, begins the same way.

THE *ATOCHA*
The Sinking

It is 1622. The *Atocha,* with its fleet of sister ships, makes its way back from South America to Spain. The *Atocha* is a treasure ship, laden with gold, jewels, silver bars, and thousands of coins.

The fleet makes a stop in Cuba and then sets off again. As the ships near Florida, a hurricane gathers strength.

Wind rips at the *Atocha*'s sails. Spray washes across the deck. The 265 people aboard the ship are terrified. Suddenly, a huge wave lifts the ship and throws it against a reef.

The hull breaks open, and the *Atocha*—along with several of its sister ships—sinks beneath the waves. All but five aboard the *Atocha* drown.

The Search

Spain wants its treasure back. Search ships are sent out. They find one of the *Atocha*'s sister ships, the *Santa Margarita*, and salvage begins. Sponge and pearl divers bring some of the *Santa Margarita*'s treasure to the surface.

But the *Atocha* cannot be found.

Hundreds of years go by. The *Atocha* is almost forgotten. Storms and strong sea currents scatter its treasure for miles along the ocean floor. The ship slowly rots and breaks into pieces. Sand covers the remains.

In the early 1960's, a new search begins. A man named Mel Fisher has read about the *Atocha*. He is determined to find the lost treasure ship. He will need boats, crew, and equipment. Investors provide the money, and the venture gets under way.

Search boats go to where it is believed the *Atocha* went down.

The boats are fitted with modern equipment for exploring the ocean bottom.

mailboxes

When the instruments register a "hit," divers go down to investigate. They keep in view of each other and regularly check their air supplies.

Large elbow-shaped pipes, called mailboxes, are swung into place. The mailboxes are Mel Fisher's invention. The whirling of the boat's propellers forces water through the mailboxes, blowing large holes in the sand. If anything is buried, it will be uncovered.

But only litter is found—nothing of value, nothing from the *Atocha*.

Where should they look next?

Mel Fisher asks for help from Eugene Lyon, an expert who can translate old Spanish documents. Lyon looks through stacks of shipping records from the 1600's. The work takes years.

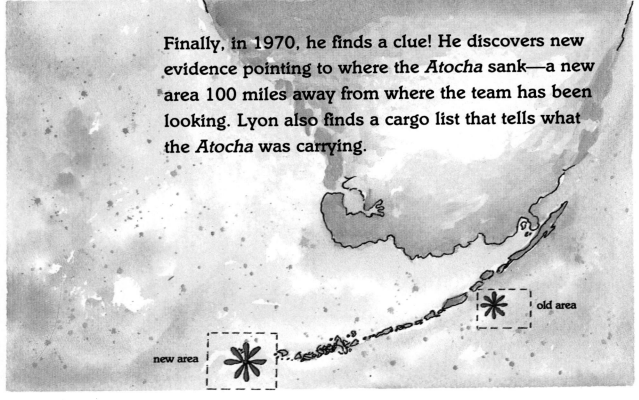

Finally, in 1970, he finds a clue! He discovers new evidence pointing to where the *Atocha* sank—a new area 100 miles away from where the team has been looking. Lyon also finds a cargo list that tells what the *Atocha* was carrying.

old area

new area

A search boat moves to the new location.

In 1971, a huge galleon anchor, several muskets, and gold bars and chains are found. But are they from the *Atocha*? There is no way to prove it.

Two years later, three heavy silver bars are recovered. The bars with their markings match up with the *Atocha*'s cargo list. Now they have proof!

Then, in 1975, the *Atocha*'s bronze cannons are found. The crew believe they are getting closer to the mother lode . . . the main treasure of the ship.

But they are wrong. Day after day they search the huge area. Many more years go by. Crew members leave and new ones sign on. When the money runs out, new investors must be found.

The Find

1985. The crew go back and search a site they had searched years ago. And then it happens—a big "hit" registers on their equipment. Divers go down.

"We found it! The mother lode!"

Mel Fisher's twenty-year search is finally over. Resting on the ocean floor, 55 feet below, is the *Atocha's* fabled treasure—glinting gold bars, jewelry, gold and silver coins, and other precious finds. Nearly all the listed cargo is there, and more—some treasure must have been smuggled aboard.

The Recording

The crew works with a marine archaeologist, Duncan Mathewson. He insists that the mother lode not be disturbed. A grid of plastic pipes is laid over the site.

underwater camera

The divers take pictures and make drawings square by square. Each square of the grid is numbered. That way the exact position of each timber, coin, and artifact is recorded.

Later, archaeologists and historians will use this information to learn about times past.

underwater slate

grid marker number 24

25

The Salvage

Now the treasure can be brought to the surface. Salvage boats are moved in. Divers descend and crew members lower baskets over the side to them.

The divers gently fan the sand with their hands and use an airlift to carefully suck it away.

airlift

As treasure is recovered, other artifacts are exposed underneath. Each piece of treasure must be accounted for. Again, everything found is sketched and photographed.

One after another, baskets full of treasure are raised to the surface.

Each day the work continues . . . dive after dive after dive. More treasure is recovered from the deep. It is hard work and can be done only in good weather.

The salvage goes on for weeks, months, and years.

Restoration and Preservation

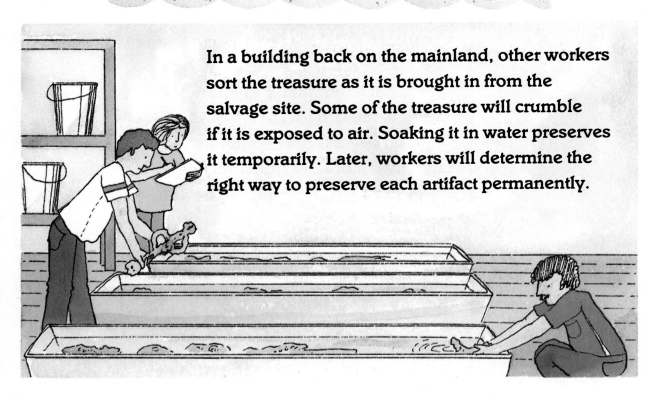

In a building back on the mainland, other workers sort the treasure as it is brought in from the salvage site. Some of the treasure will crumble if it is exposed to air. Soaking it in water preserves it temporarily. Later, workers will determine the right way to preserve each artifact permanently.

Silver coins are put into chemical baths to clean and restore them. In one or two days they will look like new.

Silver bars soak in chemical baths, too, but they will take longer to clean. They are bigger. The gold from the *Atocha* is already shiny— gold never loses its luster.

There were many pottery storage jars on board the *Atocha*. Amazingly, some are recovered whole. Other jars had been shattered and now must be pieced together again.

Cataloging

Cataloging of the *Atocha's* treasure is done in several ways:

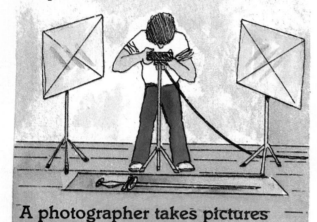

A photographer takes pictures of a sword.

Coins are scanned by a computer, and an exact description of each one is stored in the computer's memory.

An artist draws pictures of a gold plate and an emerald-studded necklace.

    This kind of careful cataloging provides a valuable record for the future.

Distribution

Some of the treasure will go to museums.

Some will go to the investors and some will go to the crew. All of them made it possible for Mel Fisher's long search to continue. A computer works out what each one's fair share will be.

The treasure of the *Nuestra Señora de Atocha* is valued at hundreds of millions of dollars . . . a very wealthy treasure ship indeed!

The wreck and its artifacts will be studied by historians and archaeologists for years to come. Their discoveries will enrich our knowledge of the past. This will be the second treasure of the *Atocha*.

ANOTHER FAMOUS TREASURE HUNT
THE MARY ROSE • an English warship

The Sinking
In 1545, the *Mary Rose*, the pride of Henry VIII's fleet, set sail to do battle against the French. She never fired a shot. Overloaded with guns and armed men, she sank off the coast of England.

The Search
In 1965, a group of British historians undertook a search for the *Mary Rose*. They knew approximately where she had gone down, but over the centuries she had been buried in sand and silt.

The Find
Two years later the *Mary Rose* was found.

The Salvage
For years divers salvaged at the site. Then, in 1982, modern equipment was used to raise the hull of the ship.

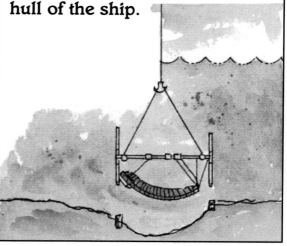

Restoration & Preservation

A special museum was built to house the hull of the *Mary Rose*. The hull must be constantly sprayed with a cold-water mist to keep the wood from disintegrating. Eventually, a waxy preserving solution will be added to the mist. The process of preservation will be completed in 2001.

Learning About the Past

The layers of mud that had settled on the *Mary Rose* preserved fragile pieces of clothing, shoes and boots. From these we know what sailors wore in 16th-century England.

By studying the hull, historians learned about shipbuilding methods at that time.

THINK IT OVER

1. Who is Mel Fisher and what does he do?

2. What kind of sailing vessel was the *Atocha*?

3. Where was the *Atocha* when the hurricane became stronger?

4. Would you want to search for sunken treasure? Why?

WRITE

Think about why finding a cargo list was important to the search. Write a radio announcement telling why the divers are certain the ship they found is the *Atocha*.

One morning I got a call from a woman named Chris Paterson. She was a friend of the archaeologist who had been searching for the *Atocha*. The treasure had been found only a few days earlier, but the search had been going on for years. "Why don't you write a book about sunken treasure?" she asked. I thought it was an exciting idea, so I called my editor, who said, "Let's do it right now."

My husband, Kent, and I went to Key West, Florida, three times. We toured the building where the treasure from the *Atocha* was being processed. I was right there as it was being lifted out of the ocean. The most amazing thing I saw really wasn't the treasure as much as the excitement and dedication of the people who found it.

What also fascinated me was the restoration process. There were people in the back of the building piecing pottery together and polishing up other pieces of the treasure. The work was highly organized, but no one knew what the divers would be bringing up next.

This mariner's astrolabe was recovered from the *Atocha* wreck site.

270

Mailboxes are used to move sand on the bottom of the ocean to uncover wrecks and treasure.

Mel Fisher has found his treasure.

I was very taken with the history of it all. For instance, one thing the divers recovered was an astrolabe, a measuring device once used in navigation. That was the kind of "treasure" that interested me the most.

At the treasure site, my husband took photographs while I asked questions. Then I drew the pictures in the book from Kent's photos. When I started *Sunken Treasure*, there was very little information on the *Atocha* search, so much of my research is original. Whenever you write nonfiction, you have to cross-check your facts. You can't just rely on information you find in other books. That's why I like to go to the source myself.

I started this kind of writing because my editor wanted more exciting nonfiction. So I wrote a book called *Clocks and How They Go*, and I found out I really liked the research part of writing. The most exciting part of nonfiction for me is taking complicated subjects and making them easy to understand. The hardest thing to make clear in *Sunken Treasure* was the gridwork process used to record the position of each piece of the treasure. Another tough part was finding pictures of past events, such as the loading of the *Atocha*, so I could re-create them as illustrations.

Gail Gibbons holds a massive gold chain recovered from the wreck of the *Atocha*.

·M·Y·S·T·E·R·I·O·U·S·
TREASURE

by Susannah Brin
and Nancy Sundquist

illustrated by
Ed Gazsi

Ships have been sailing the seven seas for thousands
of years. Over the years many ships were lost at sea.
Today, divers and treasure hunters search
the bottoms of oceans looking
for sunken ships. The deep holds
many mysteries waiting
to be solved.

Study the picture above.
How many hidden treasures can you find in the picture?

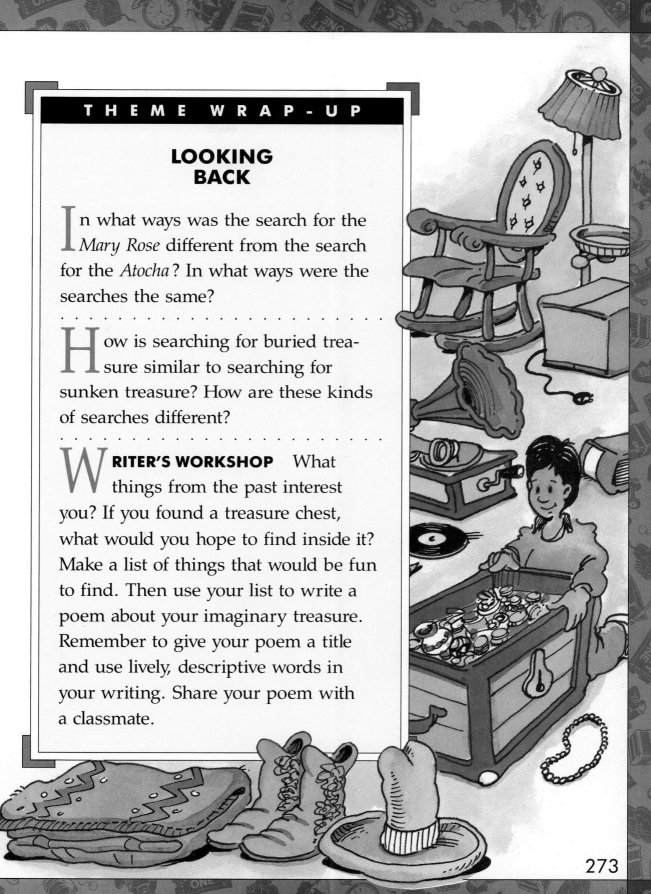

LOOKING BACK

In what ways was the search for the *Mary Rose* different from the search for the *Atocha*? In what ways were the searches the same?

. . . .

How is searching for buried treasure similar to searching for sunken treasure? How are these kinds of searches different?

. . . .

WRITER'S WORKSHOP   What things from the past interest you? If you found a treasure chest, what would you hope to find inside it? Make a list of things that would be fun to find. Then use your list to write a poem about your imaginary treasure. Remember to give your poem a title and use lively, descriptive words in your writing. Share your poem with a classmate.

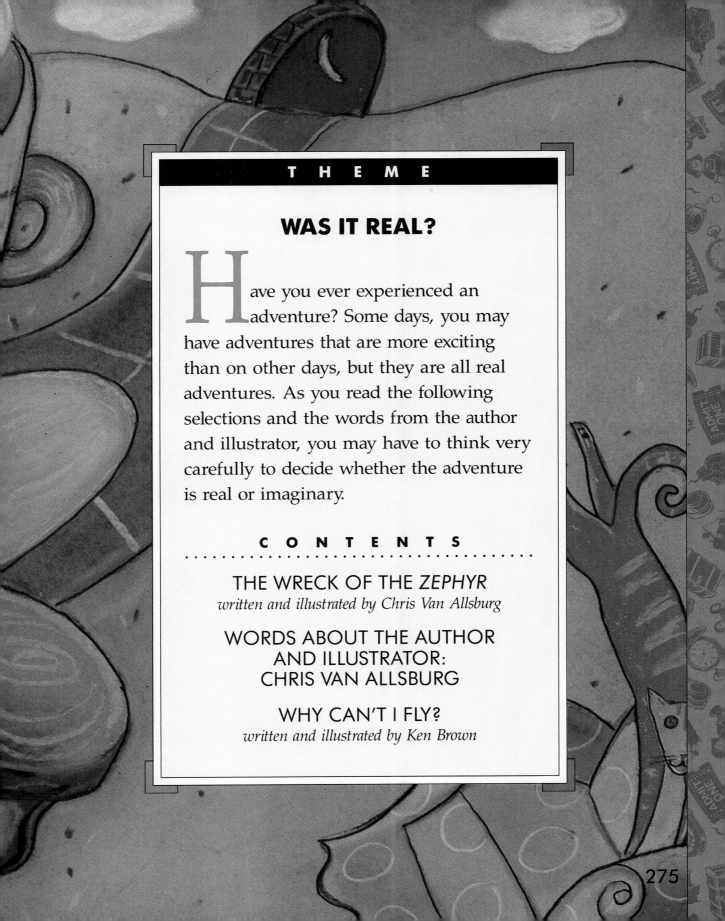

WAS IT REAL?

Have you ever experienced an adventure? Some days, you may have adventures that are more exciting than on other days, but they are all real adventures. As you read the following selections and the words from the author and illustrator, you may have to think very carefully to decide whether the adventure is real or imaginary.

C O N T E N T S

275

The Wreck of the Zephyr

The Wreck of the Zephyr

CHRIS VAN ALLSBURG

ALA NOTABLE
BOOK
CHILDREN'S CHOICE
NEW YORK TIMES
BEST ILLUSTRATED
BOOKS OF THE
YEAR

Company

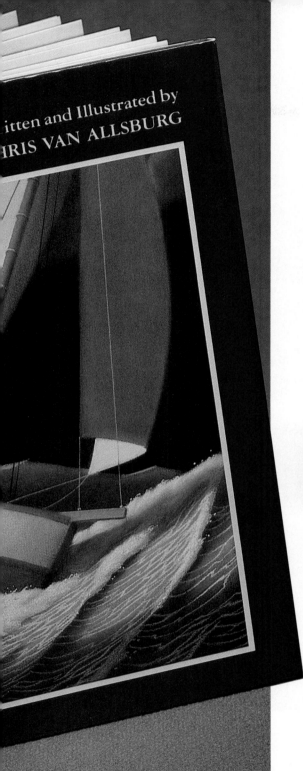

Once, while traveling along the seashore, I stopped at a small fishing village. After eating lunch, I decided to take a walk. I followed a path out of the village, uphill to some cliffs high above the sea. At the edge of these cliffs was a most unusual sight—the wreck of a small sailboat.

An old man was sitting among the broken timbers, smoking a pipe. He seemed to be reading my mind when he said, "Odd, isn't it?"

"Yes," I answered. "How did it get here?"

"Waves carried it up during a storm."

"Really?" I said. "It doesn't seem the waves could ever get that high."

Written and Illustrated by
CHRIS VAN ALLSBURG

The old man smiled. "Well, there is another story." He invited me to have a seat and listen to his strange tale.

"In our village, years ago," he said, "there was a boy who could sail a boat better than any man in the harbor. He could find a breeze over the flattest sea. When dark clouds kept other boats at anchor, the boy would sail out, ready to prove to the villagers, to the sea itself, how great a sailor he was.

"One morning, under an ominous sky, he prepared to take his boat, the *Zephyr,* out to sea. A fisherman warned the boy to stay in port. Already a strong wind was blowing. 'I'm not afraid,' the boy said, 'because I'm the greatest sailor there is.' The fisherman pointed to a sea gull gliding overhead. 'There's the only sailor who can go out on a day like this.' The boy just laughed as he hoisted his sails into a blustery wind.

"The wind whistled in the rigging as the *Zephyr* pounded her way through the water. The sky grew black and the waves rose up like mountains. The boy struggled to keep his boat from going over. Suddenly a gust of wind caught the sail. The boom swung around and hit the boy's head. He fell to the cockpit floor and did not move.

"When the boy opened his eyes, he found himself lying on a beach. The *Zephyr* rested behind him, carried there by the storm. The boat was far from the water's edge. The tide would not carry it back to sea. The boy set out to look for help.

"He walked for a long time and was surprised that he didn't recognize the shoreline. He climbed a hill, expecting to see something familiar, but what he saw instead was a strange and unbelievable sight. Before him were two boats, sailing high above the water. Astonished, he watched them glide by. Then a third sailed past, towing the *Zephyr*. The boats entered a bay that was bordered by a large village. There they left the *Zephyr*.

"The boy made his way down to the harbor, to the dock where his boat was tied. He met a sailor who smiled when he saw the boy. Pointing to the *Zephyr* he asked, 'Yours?' The boy nodded. The sailor said they almost never saw strangers on their island. It was surrounded by a treacherous reef. The *Zephyr* must have been carried over the reef by the storm. He told the boy that, later, they would take him and the *Zephyr* back over the reef. But the boy said he would not leave until he learned to sail above the waves. The sailor told him it took years to learn to sail like that. 'Besides,' he said, 'the *Zephyr* does not have the right sails.' The boy insisted. He pleaded with the sailor.

"Finally the sailor said he would try to teach him if the boy promised to leave the next morning. The boy agreed. The sailor went to a shed and got a new set of sails.

"All afternoon they sailed back and forth across the bay. Sometimes the sailor took the tiller, and the boat would magically begin to lift out of the water. But when the boy tried, he could not catch the wind that made boats fly.

"When the sun went down they went back to the harbor. They dropped anchor and a fisherman rowed them to shore. 'In the morning,' the sailor said, 'we'll put your own sails back on the *Zephyr* and send you home.' He took the boy to his house, and the sailor's wife fed them oyster stew.

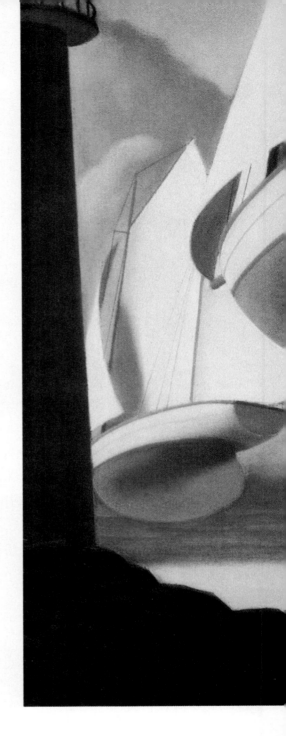

"After dinner the sailor played the concertina. He sang a song about a man named Samuel Blue, who, long ago, tried to sail his boat over land and crashed:

'For the wind o'er land's ne'er steady nor true,

an' all men that sail there'll meet Samuel Blue.'

"When he was done with his song, the sailor sent the boy to bed. But the boy could not sleep. He knew he could fly his boat if he had another chance. He waited until the sailor and his wife were asleep, then he quietly dressed and went to the harbor. As he rowed out to the *Zephyr,* the boy felt the light evening wind grow stronger and colder.

"Under a full moon, he sailed the *Zephyr* into the bay. He tried to remember everything the sailor had told him. He tried to feel the wind pulling his boat forward, lifting it up. Then, suddenly, the boy felt the *Zephyr* begin to shake. The sound of the water rushing past the hull grew louder. The air filled with spray as the boat sliced through the waves. The bow slowly began to lift. Higher and higher the *Zephyr* rose out of the water, then finally broke free. The sound of rushing water stopped. There was only the sound of wind in the sails. The *Zephyr* was flying.

"Using the stars to guide him, the boy set a course for home. The wind blew very hard, churning the sea below. But that did not matter to the *Zephyr* as she glided through the night sky. When clouds blocked the boy's view of the stars, he trimmed the sails and climbed higher. Surely the men of the island never dared fly so high. Now the boy was certain he was truly the greatest sailor of all.

"He steered well. Before the night was over, he saw the moonlit spire of the church at the edge of his village. As he drew closer to land, an idea took hold of him. He would sail over the village and ring the *Zephyr*'s bell. Then everyone would see him and know that he was the greatest sailor. He flew over the tree-topped cliffs of the shore, but as he reached the church the *Zephyr* began to fall.

"The wind had shifted. The boy pulled as hard as he could on the tiller, but it did no good. The wind shifted again. He steered for the open sea, but the trees at the cliff's edge stood between him and the water. At first there was just the rustle of leaves brushing the hull. Then the air was filled with the sound of breaking branches and ripping sails. The boat fell to the ground. And here she sits today."

"A remarkable tale," I said, as the old man stopped to relight his pipe. "What happened to the boy?"

"He broke his leg that night. Of course, no one believed his story about flying boats. It was easier for them to believe that he was lost in the storm and thrown up here by the waves." The old man laughed.

"No sir, the boy never amounted to much. People thought he was crazy. He just took odd jobs around the harbor. Most of the time he was out sailing, searching for that island and a new set of sails."

A light breeze blew through the trees. The old man looked up. "Wind coming," he said, "I've got some sailing to do." He picked up a cane, and I watched as he limped slowly toward the harbor.

THINK IT OVER

1. What unusual experiences did the boy have while he was sailing?

2. Who told the boy the tale of the *Zephyr*?

3. A fisherman told the boy that the sea gull was the only sailor that should go out on such a windy day. Explain why you think the fisherman said that.

4. What character traits did the boy have that might have led to his never amounting to much?

WRITE

Think about why the author says that the old man walked with a cane and limped. Pretend you are a doctor, and write a report explaining the reason for the old man's limp.

WORDS ABOUT THE

AUTHOR
AND
ILLUSTRATOR:

CHRIS VAN ALLSBURG

Chris Van Allsburg liked to draw when he was a boy, especially cartoon characters such as Dagwood Bumstead. But it wasn't until he went to college that he began to study art seriously. First he was a sculptor, but a friend who illustrated children's books suggested he try his hand at drawing for books, too. Van Allsburg's wife was a teacher, and she brought home books for him to look at. Then he tried one of his own. To his surprise, it was successful! Since that first book, published in 1979, Van Allsburg has become one of the most popular authors writing and drawing for young people.

Although Van Allsburg had written and illustrated two picture books before *The Wreck of the Zephyr*, this was the first book he did in color. The others had only black-and-white drawings. "Working in color is far more difficult," he says.

"When you draw in black and white, you only have to worry about how dark something is, but when there are so many different colors you can use, there's a lot more to think about. I started to work in color because it was something different and interesting."

Van Allsburg wrote *The Wreck of the Zephyr* because he wanted to do a story that took place outdoors. When he was younger, he spent a good deal of time sailing on Lake Michigan. Maybe because of that, he had a picture in his mind of a flying boat, though he says, "I'm really not sure where that image came from." After he drew the picture of the boat flying past a lighthouse, he decided to find the story behind it. Van Allsburg says *The Wreck of the Zephyr* is about possibilities—you can't be too sure what will happen in life.

Once he gets the idea for a book, it takes Van Allsburg about five months to draw the pictures and write the story. "I'm slow," he says. "I know people who make art much faster than I do. I make sketches and doodles on pieces of paper. I write story outlines. I work on what I think is the strongest idea I have at the time. I keep all the other ideas. Not in a sketchbook, though. Right now, I've got about 200 ideas floating around in my head."

Why Can't I Fly?

written and illustrated by Ken Brown

Early one morning, all the animals were gathered, as usual, by the water.

"I wish I could fly," thought the Ostrich. "Why can't I fly?" he asked the Sparrow.

"Maybe your neck is too long," suggested the Sparrow.

"The flamingoes have long necks and they can fly," replied the Ostrich, "so why can't I?"

"I don't know," chirped the Sparrow, "perhaps your legs are too long."

"The storks have long legs and they can fly," said the Ostrich, "so why can't I?"

"Well, perhaps your wings are too small," said the Sparrow.

"You've got small wings and you can fly," answered the Ostrich, "so why can't I?"

"Well, I don't know! Maybe you just don't try hard enough," and so saying, the Sparrow flew away.

"Try hard enough indeed!" thought the Ostrich. "I'll show him. I'll show all of them that I can fly." So he ran as fast as he could and, flapping his wings, he jumped off a high sand dune . . . only to land, seconds later, with a terrible thud.

Next he climbed to the top of a huge rock.

"I'll show them!" he panted.

With his wings flailing the air, he threw himself over the edge, but instantly plunged downward and landed headfirst in the soft sand below.

He remained with his head in the sand, too embarrassed to show his face.

"I'll show them!" he thought. "If my wings are too small, I'll make them bigger."

Using some large leaves, bamboo canes, strong vines, and a great deal of skill, he constructed a flying machine.

Then he climbed to the top of the high rock again, and launched himself into the air.

"This is it! Look at me, everyone. I'm flying," cried the Ostrich.

But he spoke too soon! Moments later, he landed with an almighty splash right in the middle of the river.

"Never mind," said the Sparrow. "Your long neck will keep your head well above water!"

But the Ostrich was not put off by this, his first disastrous attempt at flying. He built another flying machine with even bigger wings and once again launched himself into the air.

"Out of my way!" he shouted to the doves. "Out of my way—I'm flying!"

Alas, this flight also ended in complete disaster, when the Ostrich became totally entangled in the leaves of a high palm tree.

"Never mind!" chirped the Sparrow. "Your long legs will certainly help you to get down from there."

The Ostrich, however, was just as determined as ever to fly; he would not give up. So he built an even bigger flying machine and for the third time climbed to the top of the high rock. He took a deep breath and launched himself yet again into the air. This time, instead of plummeting straight downward as before, he soared high up into the sky, as gracefully as any other bird. "Look at me!" shouted the triumphant Ostrich. "Look, everybody, I'm flying!"

But the only reply that he got was the sound of his own voice echoing about the empty skies.

The Ostrich couldn't understand it!

"Where is everyone?" he cried. "Where's Sparrow? I'm flying and there's no one here to see. They'll never believe me now."

But they did!

THINK IT OVER

1. The Sparrow helped the Ostrich fly. What were some of the things the Sparrow said that helped the Ostrich?

2. The Ostrich wanted to fly, and he kept trying until he reached his goal. What new things have you or someone you know done over and over until they could be done well?

WRITE

Pretend you are creating a fairy tale about a flying cat or another animal that doesn't usually fly. Write a paragraph telling how the animal is able to fly.

WAS IT REAL?

Effort is often rewarded, but not always. Think about the Ostrich in "Why Can't I Fly?" and the boy in "The Wreck of the *Zephyr*." Why do you think the Ostrich is rewarded for his efforts, but not the boy?

Each of the main characters in the selections you read has different reasons for wanting to fly. Which do you think was the best reason? Which was the worst? Explain why you think as you do.

WRITER'S WORKSHOP All the characters in each of the selections you've just read have goals they want to reach. Think about your own goals. Write a journal entry describing one or more of those goals and how you plan to reach each one.

OUR NATION REMEMBERS

What building in your town contains more portraits of famous Americans than a museum or a library? The answer is—the post office!

The United States Postal Service prints new stamps several times each year. Many of these stamps honor the memories of great Americans.

These Americans have left their marks on our nation's history. Matthew A. Henson was a great explorer. Ida B. Wells was a newspaper writer. Do you recognize the other people shown?

■ Do research to find out what is special about one of these people. Share what you learn with your classmates. You may want to use the facts to make a bulletin board display.

SOCIAL STUDIES CONNECTION

MEMORIES ALL AROUND

Does your community remember its special people by naming places after them? Find out the stories behind the names. Then make a guidebook that shows these places and tells about them.

A chart like this can help you and your classmates collect facts:

What is the name of the place?	
Where is it?	
Who is it named after?	
Why is it named after this person?	

ART CONNECTION

STAMPED IN YOUR MEMORY

Draw a design for a United States stamp that shows an American you admire who is no longer living. Write a caption that tells why this person should be remembered. Display your work on a bulletin board.

Handbook

FOR

Readers and Writers

ACTIVE READING STRATEGIES

A strategy is a plan for doing something. If you practice using reading strategies, you will soon discover that you are able to read more easily. You can begin to use strategies even before you read.

The students in Kim's class have been learning how to use some reading strategies before, during, **and** after **they read.**

Before reading, Kim

✓ **previews** what she is about to read by looking through it. She reads the title and any subtitles, looks at all the pictures, and reads the captions.

✓ **thinks about what she already knows** about the subject. She reminds herself of things she has read, seen on TV, or heard about that seem connected to the topic.

✓ **predicts** what she will find out when she reads. She uses what she learned when she previewed and what she already knows about the topic to make a good guess.

✓ **sets a purpose** for reading the material. She decides whether she is reading mainly for fun or for information. She might be doing both! She knows that she might have to pay closer attention and remember details if she is reading to learn.

During reading, Kim

✓ thinks about her **predictions.** She changes them to match what she reads. Sometimes she discovers that she predicted accurately. The material confirms her predictions.

✓ asks herself **questions** about what she is reading. For example, she may want to know why the main character is afraid of horses.

✓ continues to think about **anything she already knows** or has done that is related to what she is reading. For example, she herself may be afraid of horses.

✓ makes sure she **understands** what she is reading. She stops to reread a paragraph when she realizes she doesn't really understand it.

After reading, Kim

✓ thinks again about her **predictions.** She decides how closely they matched what she read.

✓ **compares** what she learned with what she had known before about the topic. She sees that she has added to her understanding of the topic.

✓ **summarizes** what she has learned. She tells herself a few important or new ideas that she found.

READING FICTION

Fiction is writing that is made up. The author creates the characters, the setting, and the plot. You often read fiction for entertainment. You can use strategies to help you understand and remember what you read. In the example below, Carlos uses some reading strategies **before** and **during** his reading of "Song and Dance Man."

Before I read, I'll look at the pictures. I've seen people sing and dance. Who are those kids in the picture?

Song and Dance Man
by Karen Ackerman

The picture and the title of the story make me wonder if the song and dance man was on TV. I bet the story will tell me.

Grandpa was a song and dance man who once danced on the vaudeville stage.

When we visit, he tells us about a time before people watched TV, back in the good old days, the song and dance days.

"Supper in an hour!" Grandma calls from the kitchen.

"I wonder if my tap shoes still fit?" Grandpa says with a smile. Then he turns on the light to the attic, and we follow him up the steep, wooden steps.

Well, he wasn't on TV! I guess the story will tell more about vaudeville, whatever that is.

Faded posters of Grandpa when he was young hang on the walls. He moves some cardboard boxes and a rack of Grandma's winter dresses out of the way, and we see a dusty brown, leather-trimmed trunk in the corner.

As soon as Grandpa opens it, the smell of cedar chips and old things saved fills the attic. Inside are his shoes with the silver, half-moon taps on the toes and heels, bowler hats and top hats, and vests with stripes and matching bow ties.

Posters of Grandpa! He must have been famous.

We try on the hats and pretend we're dancing on a vaudeville stage, where the

bright lights twinkle and the piano player nods his head along with the music.

After wiping his shoes with a cloth he calls a shammy, Grandpa puts them on. He tucks small, white pads inside the shoes so his corns won't rub, and he turns on the lamps and aims each one down like a spotlight.

He sprinkles a little powder on the floor, and it's show time. We sit on one of Grandma's woolen blankets, clap our hands, and call out, "Yay, Grandpa!"

The song and dance man begins to dance the old soft shoe. His feet move slowly at first, while his tap shoes make soft, slippery sounds like rain on a tin roof.

We forget that it's Grandpa dancing, and all we can hear is the silvery tap of two feet, and all we can see is a song and dance man gliding across a vaudeville stage.

He says, "Watch this!" and does a new step that sounds like a woodpecker tapping on a tree. Suddenly, his shoes move faster, and he begins to sing. His voice is as round and strong as a canyon echo, and his cheeks get rosy as he sings "Yankee Doodle Boy," a song he knows from the good old days.

There are too many dance steps and too many words in the song for us to remember, but the show is better than any show on TV.

The song and dance man stops and leans forward with a wink.

"What's that in your ear?" he asks, and he pulls a silver dollar out of somebody's hair.

The story does tell more about vaudeville. It had lights and a piano player. I wonder what else happened on a vaudeville stage.

Oh, I see. I remember watching a movie about a dancer like Grandpa. I guess in vaudeville people danced this way.

The dancing sounds like a woodpecker, and the singing sounds like an echo. I can hear in my mind what this was like.

Wow! A song and dance man in vaudeville also did tricks! Vaudeville must have been really fun to see.

(See pages 234–245 for the entire story of "Song and Dance Man.")

READING NONFICTION

Nonfiction gives information and facts. It sometimes includes charts and diagrams. It may have headings and subheadings that show how the parts fit together, as in your science and social studies books.

A special study strategy known as **SQ3R** can help you read nonfiction. **S** and **Q** stand for **Survey** and **Question.** Do these steps before you read. The three **R**'s stand for **Read, Recite,** and **Review.** Here's how Sofia uses SQ3R to help her read "Sunken Treasure."

Survey means "preview." Look at the title, the headings, and the pictures. Decide what the selection is about. Think of what you already know about the topic.

This must be about wrecked treasure ships. I saw a movie about a shipwreck once.

Question yourself about what you expect to learn from your reading. Turn the title and the headings into questions. Your purpose for reading can be to find the answers.

Sunken Treasure
by Gail Gibbons

"It's there! It's really there!"
The rotting hull of a ship has been found on the ocean floor. Within the wreck lies a fabulous treasure.

The story of each underwater treasure hunt is different, but each goes back to the same beginning. . . the sinking of a ship. The story of the hunt for the *Nuestra Señora de Atocha,* a Spanish galleon, begins the same way.

The *ATOCHA*
The Sinking

It is 1622. The *Atocha,* with its fleet of sister ships, makes its way back from South America to Spain. The *Atocha* is a treasure ship, laden with gold, jewels, silver bars, and thousands of coins.

The fleet makes a stop in Cuba and then sets off again. As the ships near Florida, a hurricane gathers strength.

Wind rips at the *Atocha*'s sails. Spray washes across the deck. The 265 people aboard the ship are terrified. Suddenly, a huge wave lifts the ship and throws it against a reef.

Here are Sofia's questions.
1. What was the *Atocha*?
   How did it sink?
2. Who searched for it?
   When? Why?

Read the selection carefully. Look for answers to your questions. Reread any difficult parts.

Recite, or say in your own words, what each section is about. Here is what Sofia told herself about "The Sinking."

In 1622 the Atocha *was a ship loaded with treasure, going from South America to Spain. It sank near Florida during a hurricane.*

Review what you read by answering your questions. You may want to do this step a few days after you have read the selection. This is one way to study or prepare for a test.

The hull breaks open, and the *Atocha*—along with several of its sister ships—sinks beneath the waves. All but five aboard the *Atocha* drown.

The Search

Spain wants its treasure back. Search ships are sent out. They find one of the *Atocha*'s sister ships, the *Santa Margarita*, and salvage begins. Sponge and pearl divers bring some of the *Santa Margarita*'s treasure to the surface.

But the *Atocha* cannot be found.

Hundreds of years go by. The *Atocha* is almost forgotten. Storms and strong sea currents scatter its treasure for miles along the ocean floor. The ship slowly rots and breaks into pieces. Sand covers the remains.

In the early 1960's, a new search begins. A man named Mel Fisher has read about the *Atocha*. He is determined to find the lost treasure ship. He will need boats, crew, and equipment. Investors provide the money, and the venture gets under way.

Search boats go to where it is believed the *Atocha* went down.

The boats are fitted with modern equipment for exploring the ocean bottom.

(See pages 250–269 for the entire selection of "Sunken Treasure.")

VOCABULARY STRATEGIES

What strategies can you use to figure out a word you don't know? First, decide whether you really need to know exactly what the word means. Sometimes you will find that the meaning of the sentence or the paragraph is clear if you just keep on reading.

When you do need to know the meaning of a certain word, you can use several strategies.

- **Context clues** are often helpful. With this strategy you look for clues in the context, or words and sentences around the word you don't know.
- The **structure** of a word sometimes shows its meaning. If you know what the parts of a word mean, you can often combine them to figure out the whole word.
- If these strategies don't help, look up the word in a **glossary** or a **dictionary.**

Once you figure out the word, you'll know it when you read it again. To help yourself remember the word, write it in a vocabulary notebook. Write its meaning in your own words. You may want to add a sentence that includes the word.

Context clues and structure can show you the meanings of several words you may not know in the paragraphs on the next page.

This sentence provides you with a **context clue** for the meaning of the word *archaeologists*.

Another kind of clue may be a **definition** found near the word. The definition of *artifacts* comes right after the word.

A **synonym,** a word or a phrase that has a similar meaning, sometimes is included. *Dig up* is a synonym for *excavate*. You may even see an **antonym**, or a word that means the opposite, to give you a hint.

A **prefix** is a word part that has its own meaning. You can figure out that *restudy* means "study again" if you know that *re-* means "again."

You can probably tell what *aqualung* means from its **context,** as well as from the word *lung* that is part of it. You may even know that *aqua* means "water."

Archaeologists study ancient artifacts, which are objects made by human hands. From artifacts they learn how people lived in the past. Most archaeologists excavate, or dig up, homes, palaces, and other sites. They learn much from the artifacts as they restudy them many times.

Other archaeologists dive into the sea to bring up things from old shipwrecks. They use modern equipment, such as aqualungs that help them breathe under the water.

Archaeologists on land or in the sea don't always find gold, silver, or jewels. But nothing they find is worthless if they learn from it.

The **suffix** *-less* is a structure clue. It tells you that *worthless* means "without worth."

SPEAKING

Good speakers use strategies to help them feel more sure of themselves when they give speeches or join in discussions. Those strategies can help you, too.

- Think about your **purpose** for speaking. Is it to inform, to express, to entertain, to describe, or to persuade?
- **Prepare** what you are going to say. Even in an informal discussion, it helps to think first. For a formal speech, write notes listing your main points in order.
- **Practice.** Listen to yourself. Are you speaking slowly, clearly, and loudly enough? Check your notes as you practice. Ask someone to listen and make suggestions.

Robert plans to do a trick for his classmates and then explain how he did it. Robert knows he often forgets to explain things in the correct order. So he writes down the steps of the trick in order. As he practices, he checks his notes to help him remember.

Elena loves to listen to her father read stories aloud. She can easily picture in her mind what he is reading. She wants to read "Song and Dance Man" to her little sister, Angie.

Elena's teacher suggests that she read slowly and picture in her mind what the story describes. First, Elena reads the story to herself. She thinks about the attic and about Grandpa dancing and singing in the lamplight. As she reads aloud to Angie, she sees everything in her mind again.

LISTENING

Strategies can help you be a good listener, too. Here are some that will help you be a better listener.

- Decide what your **purpose** for listening will be. How you will listen depends on whether you want to learn something or just to relax and enjoy a story.
- **Predict** what you will hear. Check your predictions as you listen. Change them if necessary.
- **Pay attention** and try to keep track of the speaker's main points. If you need to, make some notes.

Follow Robert's and Elena's audiences as they listen.

The class enjoyed watching Robert's trick and learning how he did it. Nao wanted to do a good trick in the class talent show, so he paid close attention and even took some notes as Robert explained the trick.

Angie didn't need to learn anything from listening to Elena read "Song and Dance Man." She just wanted to enjoy it. She listened quietly and then hugged and thanked Elena when she finished reading. Elena enjoyed that!

THE WRITING PROCESS

The writing process is a strategy that will help you write better. Begin by deciding on your **task,** or the kind of writing you will do. Then select your **audience** and **purpose.** Your task might be to write a descriptive paragraph. Your audience might be your classmates, and your purpose to describe something. Now you are ready to go step by step through the writing process.

PREWRITING

First, think of a topic. It may help to brainstorm with a partner or a group. Think of something you have done, have read about, or are interested in. You might decide to write about snorkel diving in Florida.

Your next step is to organize your ideas. You can do this by making a list of events in order, a story map, a drawing, or an outline. For a description, try a web diagram with the topic in the center and details around it.

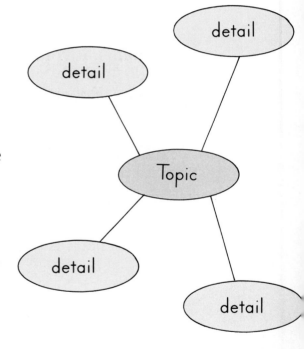

DRAFTING

These strategies may help you write your first draft:

- Use your list or diagram so you include all your details.
- Get your ideas down on paper. Make corrections later.

Remember that at the end of each step you can decide to move to the next step or go back and start over again.

RESPONDING AND REVISING

When you ask your writing partner or group to respond to your draft, here are some suggestions your partner or group might make to improve your writing.

- Change the first sentence so that it states the topic.
- Use words and details that help people see, feel, and hear what you are describing.
- Combine two short sentences to make a better one.

Remember that you don't have to follow all the advice you get. Change only what you think will improve your writing.

Imagine that you wrote this draft describing a snorkel-diving experience. Notice the way editor's marks show some of the changes you might make to improve it.

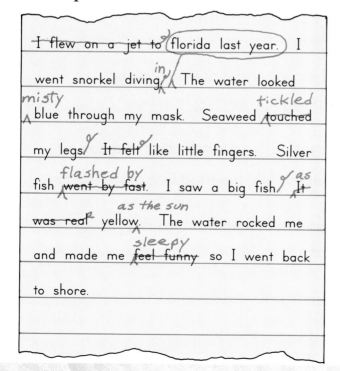

EDITOR'S MARKS	
∧	Add something.
✄	Cut something.
♂	Move something.
∧	Replace something.

PROOFREADING

After revising your paragraph, you are ready to correct errors. As you proofread, use more editor's marks.

EDITOR'S MARKS	
☰	Use a capital letter.
⊙	Add a period.
⋀	Add a comma.
ＶＶ	Add quotation marks.
↺	Transpose.
◯	Spell correctly.
ℋ	Indent paragraph.
⁄	Make a lowercase letter.

Check for the following things as you proofread.

✓ Did you indent your paragraph? Use this mark: ℋ .

✓ Did you capitalize names? Use this mark: ☰ .

ℋ I went snorkel diving in florida last year.

✓ Did you circle misspelled words and write the correct spelling above? Add them to your spelling notebook.

✓ Did you begin each sentence with a capital letter and end it with the correct punctuation? Add a period like this: ⊙ .

✓ Did you check grammar and punctuation? Use this mark for a missing comma: ⋀ .

The water rocked me and made me sleepy, so I went back to shore.

PUBLISHING

Now it's time to share your writing with your audience. When you have made all the corrections, copy the paragraph in your best handwriting. Letting your audience read your paragraph is one way to publish it. You may want to publish it in some other way. Here are some ways you could publish your description of snorkel diving.

- Make a travel poster for Florida. Write the words "Come to Florida" in big letters at the top of a piece of poster board. Draw an illustration of your description. Attach your paragraph.

- Read your description aloud to the class. Show your equipment and how to use it. Leave time for questions from your audience. You're the expert!

- Make a bulletin board display of the underwater world, using your paragraph. Add drawings and photographs.

RESEARCHING INFORMATION

You can use several strategies to get information for a research report. You can **skim, scan**, and **take notes.** If your research topic is famous shipwrecks, the librarian might suggest *The Titanic: Lost ... and Found* by Judy Donnelly.

Skimming means looking over a book or selection quickly to find out how it is organized and what it is about. **Scanning** means looking quickly to find certain information.

You could skim the book to find where it tells what happened to the ship.

To find how many people were on the ship, you could scan for that number.

> **Chapter 3**
> ### Never Again
> Soon the news flashes all around the world. The unsinkable *Titanic* has sunk. More than 2,200 people set out. Only 705 are rescued.
> How? Why? No one can understand.

Take notes to help remember the information you find.

Write the main idea as a question at the top of a note card.

Write only what you need to remember. Use your own words. You don't need to write whole sentences.

Write where you found the information.

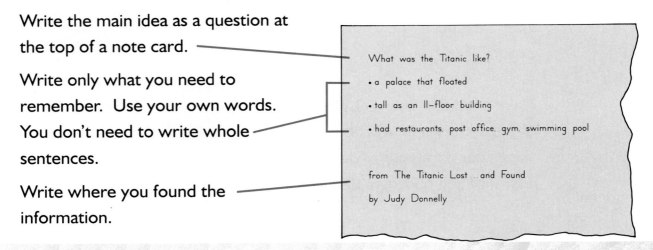

What was the Titanic like?
- a palace that floated
- tall as an 11-floor building
- had restaurants, post office, gym, swimming pool

from The Titanic Lost ... and Found
by Judy Donnelly

THE PARTS OF A BOOK

Most books, like this one, contain special pages that will help you find the information you want.

These pages are all at the front of the book.

The **title page** tells the title of the book, the author's name, and the company that published the book.

The **copyright page** tells when the book was published and often other important facts.

Some books have a **dedication**. This is a statement by the author thanking someone.

The **table of contents** lists the chapters in the book and tells the page number on which each chapter begins.

Table of Contents

A glossary and an index usually come at the end of the book.

Glossary

A **glossary** is like a dictionary. It tells meanings of certain words as they are used in the book. The words are listed in alphabetical order.

An **index** lists topics in the book in alphabetical order and gives the pages where each is mentioned.

Index

THE LIBRARY

Whether you are looking for information or for a book to read for pleasure, a library is the place to find it.

Start with the **card catalog.** It holds cards that describe every book in the library. They are filed in alphabetical order by the first word on the card. Sometimes the card catalog is part of a data base on microfilm or on a computer. Because different libraries use different kinds of computer systems, you may need to ask the librarian to help you get started. The computer often provides directions that are easy to follow.

In a standard card catalog, each book has three different cards—a title card, an author card, and a subject card. Each nonfiction book has a **call number,** which is written on its cards, on the library shelf, and on the book itself. Fiction books have letters from the author's last name instead of numbers.

The title card lists the title of the book first.

The author card lists the author's last name first.

The subject card lists the subject of the book first.

The Titanic.
J   Donnelly, Judy.
910.4

Donnelly, Judy.
J   The Titanic: lost . . . and found /
910.4

TITANIC (STEAMSHIP)
J   Donnelly, Judy.
910.4   The Titanic: lost. . . and found /
        Donnelly, Judy;
        Illustrated by Keith Kohler.
        New York : Random House,
        ©1987.

Libraries are organized into several different sections. They often have a special area for children's books. Here, books are grouped in sections such as picture books, fiction, and nonfiction. Sometimes books that are easy to read or books about a topic such as horses or sports are found on special tables or shelves.

Encyclopedias, dictionaries, almanacs, and atlases are kept in the **reference section** of a library. Usually these items cannot be checked out because many people need to use them.

Encyclopedias contain information on topics that are arranged in alphabetical order. Each volume, or book, in the encyclopedia is labeled with the letters of the topics it includes. At the end of the article about each topic is a list of other topics related to it. Encyclopedias often have a separate volume that is an index.

Some libraries also have encyclopedias that are data bases on laser disks or computers. The librarian can help you use these electronic encyclopedias. Information on these data bases is usually organized in alphabetical order by topic, too.

The best sources for information on current events are **magazines** and **newspapers.** These have their own place in the library. The newest magazines cannot be taken out, but sometimes older ones can. Old newspapers are often saved on microfilm. If you know the date of the newspaper you want to see, the librarian will give you the microfilm and show you how to use the microfilm reader machine.

GLOSSARY

The **pronunciation** of each word in this glossary is shown by a phonetic respelling in brackets; for example, [ə·kā′zhən·əl·ē]. An accent mark (′) follows the syllable with the most stress: [kun′ing]. A secondary, or lighter, accent mark (′) follows a syllable with less stress: [par′ə·sho͞ot′]. The key to other pronunciation symbols is below. You will find a shortened version of this key on alternate pages of the glossary.

Pronunciation Key*

a	add, map	m	move, seem	u	up, done
ā	ace, rate	n	nice, tin	û(r)	burn, term
â(r)	care, air	ng	ring, song	yo͞o	fuse, few
ä	palm, father	o	odd, hot	v	vain, eve
b	bat, rub	ō	open, so	w	win, away
ch	check, catch	ô	order, jaw	y	yet, yearn
d	dog, rod	oi	oil, boy	z	zest, muse
e	end, pet	ou	pout, now	zh	vision, pleasure
ē	equal, tree	o͝o	took, full	ə	the schwa,
f	fit, half	o͞o	pool, food		an unstressed
g	go, log	p	pit, stop		vowel representing
h	hope, hate	r	run, poor		the sound spelled
i	it, give	s	see, pass		a in *above*
ī	ice, write	sh	sure, rush		e in *sicken*
j	joy, ledge	t	talk, sit		i in *possible*
k	cool, take	th	thin, both		o in *melon*
l	look, rule	t̶h̶	this, bathe		u in *circus*

*Adapted entries, the Pronunciation Key, and the Short Key that appear on the following pages are reprinted from *HBJ School Dictionary*. Copyright © 1990 by Harcourt Brace Jovanovich, Inc. Reprinted by permission of Harcourt Brace Jovanovich, Inc.

acacia

alfalfa The Arabs of the Middle East grew a plant they called *al-facfacah*, which meant "the best kind of food for cattle and horses." The Spanish people called it *alfalfez*. When the Europeans settled in North and South America, they brought it with them.

anchor

A

a·board [ə·bôrd'] *prep.* On, in, or into: **Everyone** *aboard* **the plane enjoyed seeing wonderful views of the Grand Canyon from the air.**

a·ca·cia [ə·kā'shə] *n.* A tree with yellow flowers, found in warm areas: **All the** *acacia* **trees died during the rare cold spell.**

a·cre [ā'kər] *n.* An area of land that is as big as a square with sides about 210 feet long: **One square mile is as big as 640** *acres.*

a·gent [ā'jənt] *n.* A person who acts with instructions from someone else; a person who represents a group: **The FBI** *agent* **spent a month following and watching the spy who lived in the house across the street.**

al·fal·fa [al·fal'fə] *n.* A plant with purple flowers, used to feed horses and cows: **The farmer stored piles of** *alfalfa* **in the barn to feed the cows and horses in the winter.**

a·maze·ment [ə·māz'mənt] *n.* Great surprise or wonder: **In** *amazement,* **Lenora watched her friend finish all the math problems in ten minutes.**

an·chor [ang'kər] *n.* A heavy piece of metal tied to a boat and dropped to the bottom of the water to keep the boat from moving: **The sailor forgot to throw the** *anchor* **over the side, so during the night the boat moved four miles from the shore.**

arch·er fish [är'chər fish] *n.* A small fish that catches insects by stunning them with drops of water it squirts from its mouth.

ar·ti·fact [är'tə·fakt'] *n.* Something made by humans: **The most interesting** *artifact* **the explorer found was a carved wooden box.**

ar·ti·fi·cial [är'tə·fish'əl] *adj.* Made by a human; fake: **The juice had** *artificial* **flavors added to it, so it didn't taste at all like real orange juice.**

at·tic [at′ik] *n.* The top floor of a house, right under the roof: **The twins liked to play up in the *attic* so they could hear the squirrels running across the roof.**

at·tract [ə·trakt′] *v.* **at·tract·ed, at·tract·ing** To grab the attention of someone or something; to cause someone or something to come near: **The baby was *attracted* to my silver bracelet and crawled over for a closer look.**

awl [ôl] *n.* A pointed tool used to punch holes in wood or leather: **My grandfather used an *awl* to make holes in my new leather belt.**

B

ba·bush·ka [bə·bŏŏsh′kə] *n.* A scarf worn on the head: **Dana always wore a wool *babushka* in the winter because it kept her head warm.**

bac·te·ria [bak·tir′ē·ə] *n. pl.* One-celled living things too small to see without a microscope: **Although *bacteria* are much too small to see, some of them can cause diseases.**

bam·boo [bam·bŏŏ′] *adj.* Made of a tall grass with hard, hollow stems: **All the furniture in the house was made of oak except for the beautiful *bamboo* table in front of the sofa.**

ban·dit [ban′dit] *n.* A robber: **The *bandit* opened the gate and stole the fastest horses from the king's stables.**

bar·ri·er [bar′ē·ər] *n.* Something blocking the way: **The fat little puppy tried to climb over the *barrier* at the door so it could get out of the kitchen.**

bed·roll [bed′rōl′] *n.* A sleeping bag or a thin mattress that is rolled up: **Tran always brought an extra blanket to use with his *bedroll* so he would be warm when he slept.**

babushka It may surprise you to learn that the Russian word for "grandmother" is *babushka*. When we use this word in America, we usually mean "a scarf worn on the head." This kind of head covering was often worn by older women who came to America from Russia and eastern Europe.

bamboo

a	add	o͞o	took
ā	ace	o͞o	pool
â	care	u	up
ä	palm	û	burn
e	end	yo͞o	fuse
ē	equal	oi	oil
i	it	ou	pout
ī	ice	ng	ring
o	odd	th	thin
ō	open	th	this
ô	order	zh	vision

ə = { a in *above*   e in *sicken*   i in *possible*   o in *melon*   u in *circus* }

boa

bowler

be·lat·ed [bi·lā′tid] *adj.* Too late: **Amy's *belated* birthday card arrived in the mail six days after Jan's birthday.**

bel·low [bel′ō] *v.* **bel·lowed, bel·low·ing** To roar or cry out: **The cows in the field started *bellowing* loudly when it began to thunder.**

bleak [blēk] *adj.* Cold, harsh, and gloomy: **Tonio hated to get out of bed on *bleak* winter mornings.**

blun·der [blun′dər] *v.* **blun·dered, blun·der·ing** To stumble; to move stupidly: **When the lights went out, Kim *blundered* across the dark room and almost tripped over a stool.**

blus·ter·y [blus′tər·ē] *adj.* Blowing strongly: **The cold *blustery* wind blew snow into Ronnie's face.**

boa [bō′ə] *n.* A long scarf made of feathers or fur: **Mrs. Brown liked to wear her feather *boa* because it kept her neck warm.**

bolt [bōlt] *n.* A metal screw or pin used with a nut to hold something in place: **Kim and his sister used two small *bolts* to fasten the new bell to his bicycle.**

bore [bôr] *v.* **bored, bor·ing** To make someone feel uninterested and tired of something: **The children were *bored* on Saturday afternoon because they had nothing to do.**

bou·quet [bō·kā′ or bōō·kā′] *n.* A bunch of flowers: **Wanda picked a huge *bouquet* of tulips and other spring flowers for her sister's seventh birthday.**

bow [bō] *n.* A curved piece of wood used with a string to shoot arrows: **Even though her *bow* broke when she shot the arrow, Nixia was able to hit the target right in the center.**

bowl·er [bō′lər] *adj.* Like a round, hard hat made of felt: **Dwayne sat on his grandfather's *bowler* hat, squashing it so Grandpa couldn't wear it anymore.**

brit·tle [brit′(ə)l] *adj.* Easily broken or snapped: **The candy was so *brittle* that it broke into a hundred pieces in her mouth.**

browse [brouz] *v.* To feed on leaves and twigs: **The cows, sheep, and horses *browse* quietly in the fields every afternoon in the summer.** *syn.* graze

car·go [kär′gō] *n.* The goods carried by a boat or a plane: **They unloaded the bananas and coffee from the *cargo* hold of the ship from South America.**

cat·a·log [kat′ə·lôg′ *or* kat′ə·log′] *v.* **cat·a·loged, cat·a·log·ing** To make a list of names and objects with a description of each one: **The librarian is *cataloging* the library's new books each month.**

ce·dar [sē′dər] *adj.* Made of the reddish wood of a large evergreen tree: **Mrs. Kane made a *cedar* chest to keep all her woolen blankets in.**

chauf·feur [shō′fər *or* shō·fûr′] *n.* Someone paid to drive a car: **Mr. Gordon hired a *chauffeur* to drive his car so he could work on the way to his office.**

chuck·le [chuk′əl] *v.* To laugh softly: **When Andrew heard the raccoon *chuckle*, he thought it was Paul laughing.**

churn [chûrn] *v.* **churned, churn·ing** To move about with force: **The motor was *churning* the water into white foam behind the boat.**

clam·or [klam′ər] *n.* A loud, steady noise: **The animals in the zoo made such a *clamor* at feeding time that people could not hear each other talk.**

clear·ing [klir′ing] *n.* A small area without trees in a forest: **The campers slept soundly in a small *clearing* brightened by moonlight.**

chauffeur

chauffeur Would you believe that a *chauffeur* once kept a car's engine warm by tending a fire? At one time automobiles were driven by steam engines. One of the driver's jobs was to keep the water in the boiler hot enough to make the steam that powered the car. The word *chauffeur* comes from the French word *chauffer*, which means "to heat."

clearing

a	add	o͞o	took
ā	ace	o͞o	pool
â	care	u	up
ä	palm	û	burn
e	end	yo͞o	fuse
ē	equal	oi	oil
i	it	ou	pout
ī	ice	ng	ring
o	odd	th	thin
ō	open	th	this
ô	order	zh	vision

ə = { a in *above* e in *sicken*
i in *possible*
o in *melon* u in *circus* }

client *Client* comes to us from the Latin language spoken by the ancient Romans. A *client* was originally a person who "depended on" someone else. Today, a *client* depends on another person for help or a service and pays money for it.

cockpit

concertina

cli·ent [klī′ənt] *n.* A customer or a person who looks for professional help: **On television shows, a private detective often seems to work for only one *client*.**

cock·pit [kok′pit′] *n.* A low part in a boat where the driver sits: **The Coast Guard officer jumped into the *cockpit* and started the motor.**

con·cer·ti·na [kon′sər·tē′nə] *n.* A small musical instrument that is squeezed and pulled apart to make music: **Don played such lively music on his *concertina* that we all wanted to dance.**

con·gress·man [kong′gris·mən] *n.* A member of the United States Congress who is a man: **The *congressmen* asked the congresswoman from Colorado if she agreed with them.**

con·sume [kən·sōōm′] *v.* **con·sumed, con·sum·ing** To destroy completely: **The fire was *consuming* the house so quickly that we knew nothing would be left.**

co·or·di·nate [kō·ôr′də·nāt′] *v.* **co·or·di·nat·ed, co·or·di·nat·ing** To make the parts of something work together: **Molly carefully *coordinated* the plans for the picnic to make sure everyone would bring something that we needed.**

corn [kôrn] *n.* A sore that sometimes grows on toes where shoes rub against them: **She had so many painful *corns* on her feet that she wore soft slippers in the house.**

cous·in [kuz′(ə)n] *n.* The son or daughter of your uncle or aunt: **Even though I have six aunts and uncles, I only have one *cousin*.**

cre·ate [krē·āt′] *v.* **cre·at·ed, cre·at·ing** To make: **Latoya *created* a farm scene with animals made from clay.**

cun·ning [kun′ing] *adj.* Clever: **The fox was so *cunning* that it was able to undo the door to its cage and escape.** *syn.* tricky

cy·cle [sī′kəl] *n.* Events that happen in the same order, over and over again: **One of the *cycles* of nature is that of the seasons—spring, summer, fall, and winter.**

D

dart [därt] *n.* A small weapon like a tiny arrow that can be shot from a gun or thrown by hand: **Suzy's dad showed her how to throw the *darts* safely so that they would land in the center of the target.**

disc [disk] *n.* A flat circle: **As the plastic *disc* went spinning through the air, the dog leaped and caught it in his jaws.**

dis·guise [dis·gīz′] *v.* **dis·guised, dis·guis·ing** To change the way something looks: **Rachel *disguised* herself so well that no one knew who she was.**

dis·may [dis·mā′] *n.* Surprised unhappiness: **Ann felt *dismay* when she saw that her favorite playground was now a parking lot.**

doc·u·ment [dok′yə·mənt] *n.* A written paper that proves something or gives information: **Mrs. Ivan kept in a locked box the *documents* that proved she was an American citizen.**

drought [drout] *n.* A long period without rain: **We need rain to end the *drought* and save the crops.**

E

ea·ger·ly [ē′gər·lē] *adv.* With great interest or excitement.

ech·o [ek′ō] *n.* A sound that repeats as it bounces back from a solid object: **Gabe heard the *echo* of his name after he shouted it into the canyon.**

e·co·sys·tem [ek′ō·sis′təm] *n.* The living things and nonliving surroundings in an area that work together and affect each other: **Cutting down trees can upset the *ecosystem* of a forest so much that it will rain less and many animals will die.**

dart

document

drought *Drought* and *dry* both come from the Old English word *dryge.* This makes sense because a *drought* is "a long period of time without rain." Although *drought* ends like *thought,* say it so that it rhymes with *out.*

a	add	o͞o	took
ā	ace	o͞o	pool
â	care	u	up
ä	palm	û	burn
e	end	yo͞o	fuse
ē	equal	oi	oil
i	it	ou	pout
ī	ice	ng	ring
o	odd	th	thin
ō	open	th	this
ô	order	zh	vision

ə = { a in *above*   e in *sicken*
     i in *possible*
     o in *melon*   u in *circus* }

embrace

fleet

ee·rie [ir′ē] *adj.* Weird, strange: **An *eerie* noise somewhere in the old house woke up Lydia from a sound sleep.**

em·brace [im·brās′] *v.* **em·braced, em·brac·ing** To hug: **Marie *embraced* the dog so hard that he yelped and tried to squirm away from her.**

en·gaged [in·gājd′] *adj.* Planning to be married: **My sister is *engaged* to marry a boy she met twenty years ago when they were in kindergarten.**

ev·i·dence [ev′ə·dəns] *n.* Proof that something is true or false: **The thief's fingerprints on the glass were clear *evidence* that he had been in the house.**

F

fi·na·le [fə·nä′lē] *n.* The last part of a show: **The concert ended with a grand *finale* that included beautiful fireworks.**

fish [fish] *v.* **fished, fish·ing** To try to get something from someone: **Although he kept saying that he hadn't played well, we knew Patrick was *fishing* for praise.**

fla·vor [flā′vər] *n.* A special taste or quality: **The clowns gave a circus *flavor* to the party.**

fleet [flēt] *n.* A group of ships from the same country or company: **The small *fleet* of fishing ships filled the harbor.**

flur·ry [flûr′ē] *v.* **flur·ried, flur·ry·ing** To blow or stir around suddenly: **Mike tried to rake the leaves *flurrying* in the wind, but it seemed impossible.**

fren·zy [fren′zē] *n.* A wild fit or effort: **She cleaned up her room in a *frenzy*, trying to finish before she had to leave for the hockey game.**

fuel [fyo͞o′əl] *n.* Something that burns easily to create heat or energy: **Mr. Wang used logs and paper as *fuel* when he built a fire in the fireplace.**

fun·gus [fung′gəs] *n.* A plant with no leaves or flowers, such as a mushroom: **The mushrooms that grow up suddenly in the grass after a rainstorm are a kind of** *fungus.*

fur·ry [fûr′ē] *adj.* Covered with hair: **The kitten yawned and curled up beside the** *furry* **belly of his mother.**

G

gal·le·on [gal′ē·ən] *n.* A large sailing ship of earlier times: **The divers found a sunken** *galleon* **still loaded with its rich cargo of gold bars, coins, and jewels.**

gar·lic [gär′lik] *n.* A plant like an onion with a strong taste and smell, often used to flavor food: **Bread toasted with butter and** *garlic* **is often served with a dinner of spaghetti and meatballs.**

ging·ko [ging′kō *or* jing′kō] *n.* A kind of large tree with fan-shaped leaves, found in Asia and the United States: **Her silver earrings were made in the fanlike shape of leaves from the** *gingko* **tree.**

glance [glans] *v.* To look quickly.

gran·ite [gran′it] *n.* A kind of hard rock often used to make buildings: **The houses in the seaport were made of** *granite* **so that fierce storms couldn't destroy them.**

gust [gust] *n.* A quick rush of wind: **A** *gust* **of wind suddenly blew her hat off her head.**

H

half-moon [haf′mo͞on′] *adj.* Shaped like an arc or like the moon when only part of it can be seen: **George drew cartoon people with** *half-moon* **eyes, so they always looked sleepy.**

galleon

gingko The *gingko* tree was first planted in the United States about 1780. The name *gingko* is Japanese, because the tree grew first in Japan, Korea, and China. The gingko is the oldest kind of tree still in existence. It lived through the Ice Age, which destroyed other kinds of trees.

half-moon

a	add	o͞o	took
ā	ace	o͞o	pool
â	care	u	up
ä	palm	û	burn
e	end	yo͞o	fuse
ē	equal	oi	oil
i	it	ou	pout
ī	ice	ng	ring
o	odd	th	thin
ō	open	th	this
ô	order	zh	vision

ə = { a in *above*　e in *sicken*　i in *possible*　o in *melon*　u in *circus* }

har·bor [här′bər] *n.* A safe place near the edge of the water, where boats put down their anchors: **In the afternoon, the sailors climbed aboard their ships, which were waiting in the** *harbor.* *syn.* port

haul [hôl] *v.* **hauled, haul·ing** To move or carry: **After** *hauling* **furniture up to our new apartment, we were so tired that we fell asleep.**

hemp [hemp] *adj.* Like, or made of, the fibers of a tall plant with small green flowers, used to make rope: **The fishermen used** *hemp* **ropes to make their nets strong enough to hold large fish.**

incline

hitch [hich] *v.* **hitched, hitch·ing** To tie something to something else: **The settlers carefully** *hitched* **the horses to the wagon before they left their camp.**

hoist [hoist] *v.* **hoist·ed, hoist·ing** To raise: **The sailor** *hoisted* **the flag on our boat to let the other ship know where we came from.**

hull [hul] *n.* The body of a ship: **The ship's** *hull* **cracked when the storm drove it onto the rocks.**

i·de·a [ī·dē′ə] *n.* A thought: **Tammy had a good** *idea* **for what to do at the picnic.**

in·cline [in′klīn] *n.* A slope or a steep surface: **The hill where we go sledding is a steep** *incline* **from top to bottom.**

in·vest·or [in·vest′ər] *n.* Someone who spends money on something that might bring more money later: **Ten** *investors* **paid for building the amusement park, hoping to make millions of dollars after it opened.**

lad·en [lād′(ə)n] *adj.* Loaded: *Laden* **with books and papers, Carlos could hardly get up the stairs.**

latch [lach] *v.* To fasten something shut: **Walter didn't *latch* the gate, so the dog pushed it open and ran away.**

lim·o [lim'ō] *n. informal* A limousine or a very large car: **The performers drove up to the theater in a shiny black *limo*.**

limp [limp] *adj.* Without stiffness; not firm: **It was hard to turn the *limp* pages of the wet newspapers.**

lope [lōp] *v.* **loped, lop·ing** To run with long, slow steps: **As the mule came *loping* along the path, Charlie was able to run and catch it.**

lus·ter [lus'tər] *n.* Shine; brightness: **Eric polished the silver to give it *luster*.**

M

ma·neu·ver [mə·n(y)ōō'vər] *v.* **ma·neu·vered, ma·neu·ver·ing** To move something with skill: **Mrs. Nikos *maneuvered* the car around the bicycles and toys in the driveway.**

marsh [märsh] *n.* A low place where the ground is wet and swampy: **You need to wear waterproof boots when you go out to look for birds in the *marshes* near the river.** *syns.* swamp, bog

mask [mask] *n.* Something that covers or hides a face or its expressions: **She covered her face with a *mask* that matched her costume perfectly.**

may·or [mā'ər] *n.* The person in charge of a town: **The *mayors* of ten cities met to talk about improving roads between the cities.**

mead·ow [med'ō] *n.* A field where wild grass grows but few trees: **The children tried to play a game of soccer in the *meadow*, but they kept losing the ball in the grass.**

mi·grate [mī'grāt'] *v.* **mi·grat·ed, mi·grat·ing** To move from one area to settle in another: **Year after year, the geese had *migrated* south to avoid the cold winters.**

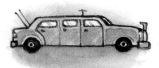
limo

mask

meadow

a	add	o͞o	took
ā	ace	o͞o	pool
â	care	u	up
ä	palm	û	burn
e	end	yo͞o	fuse
ē	equal	oi	oil
i	it	ou	pout
ī	ice	ng	ring
o	odd	th	thin
ō	open	th	this
ô	order	zh	vision

ə = { a in *above* e in *sicken* i in *possible* o in *melon* u in *circus* }

mush·y [mush'ē] *adj.* Very soft and easy to squeeze: **The banana was so ripe and** *mushy* **that it oozed from the peel.** *syn.* squashy

mushy

mut·ter [mut'ər] *v.* **mut·tered, mut·ter·ing** To say something unclearly and in a low voice without completely opening your mouth: **Stan** *muttered* **as he recited the alphabet to himself.**

N

ner·vous [nûr'vəs] *adj.* Very worried and a little scared: **The thunder and rain made the people at our picnic** *nervous* **for a while.**

nim·ble [nim'bəl] *adj.* Able to move easily and quickly: **Meg was so** *nimble* **and strong that she was good at gymnastics.**

nut

ni·tro·gen [nī'trə·jən] *n.* A substance that is necessary for life: **Farmers sometimes add** *nitrogen* **to the soil so plants will grow better.**

noc·tur·nal [nok·tûr'nəl] *adj.* Active at night: *Nocturnal* **animals, such as raccoons and bats, sleep during the day.**

nour·ish [nûr'ish] *v.* **nour·ished, nour·ish·ing** To feed; to keep healthy or to make something grow with food: **The milk** *nourished* **the lost kittens, helping them grow two inches in two weeks.**

nut [nut] *n.* A small piece of metal with a hole in it, used to hold a bolt in place: *Nuts* **screw onto the ends of bolts to hold things together.**

nu·tri·ent [n(y)ōō'trē·ənt] *n.* The useful part of food: **Mr. Perez told us we would be healthier if we ate food that has the right** *nutrients.*

O

oc·ca·sion·al·ly [ə·kā'zhən·əl·ē] *adv.* Sometimes; once in a while: *Occasionally,* **Mr. Lee showed a movie in science class.**

of·fi·cial [ə·fish'əl] *n.* A person who is in charge of something: **Health *officials* warned parents about the measles outbreak.**

om·i·nous [om'ə·nəs] *adj.* Looking or sounding as if something bad or scary will happen: **The sky looked black and *ominous* before the heavy thunderstorm brought rain.**

owl·ing [oul'ing] *n.* The act of searching for owls: **When we went *owling* with our grandfather, all we saw were bats.**

P

par·a·chute [par'ə·sho͞ot'] *v.* **par·a·chut·ed, par·a·chut·ing** To slow a person's fall toward the ground by using a parachute, which is a large, umbrella-shaped piece of material, attached to the body with straps: **When they jump from an airplane, *parachuting* firefighters have to be careful where they land.**

par·ka [pär'kə] *n.* A winter coat with a hood: **Gail loved the *parka* with the warm wool lining because her aunt had given it to her.**

pent·house [pent'hous'] *n.* An apartment on the top floor of a building: **From that *penthouse* in the middle of New York City, you can clearly see the Statue of Liberty.**

pi·an·o [pē·an'ō] *n.* An instrument played by hitting its keys with the fingers to create music: **The old *piano* was missing some keys, so the player had to skip some notes of the song, but we didn't care.**

pierce [pirs] *v.* **pierced, pierc·ing** To poke through with something pointed: **The sharp tree branch *pierced* a hole in the knee of Brett's brand-new jeans.**

pipe [pīp] *v.* **piped, pip·ing** To speak in a high voice: **While the grown-ups were talking about cooking the turkey, Emma *piped* up that she smelled something burning.**

parachute Did you know that there were parachutes before there were airplanes? As early as 1785, people used parachutes to escape from hot-air balloons that were in trouble.

parka

piano The Italian man who made the first piano in 1711 was proud of his invention. The best and most unusual thing about it was that it could be played both *piano e forte*. In Italian this means "soft and loud."

a	add	o͞o	took
ā	ace	o͞o	pool
â	care	u	up
ä	palm	û	burn
e	end	yo͞o	fuse
ē	equal	oi	oil
i	it	ou	pout
ī	ice	ng	ring
o	odd	th	thin
ō	open	th	this
ô	order	zh	vision

ə = { a in *above*　e in *sicken*　i in *possible*　o in *melon*　u in *circus* }

pizza

port

propeller

piz·za [pēt′sə] *n.* A baked flat crust covered with cheese, tomato sauce, and other food: **Gina made a huge *pizza* crust and then covered it with tomato sauce and cheese.**

pluck [pluk] *v.* To pull off or pull out: **Steve wanted to *pluck* some daisies from the field to give to his grandmother.**

plum·met [plum′it] *v.* **plum·met·ed, plum·met·ing** To fall straight down: **The wind had stopped, and the kite was *plummeting* toward the ground.**

plump [plump] *adj.* A little fat: **He bought a *plump* chicken to cook for dinner.**

port [pôrt] *n.* A place where ships come to and leave from: **The *port* was so small that there was room for only ten boats.** *syn.* harbor

pre·cious [presh′əs] *adj.* Worth a great deal of money; valued by someone: **The thief took only *precious* gems from the store, leaving less valuable jewelry behind.**

pre·serve [pri·zûrv′] *v.* To keep something in its original form: **A camper who cares about nature *preserves* the park by not littering and by putting out campfires carefully.**

pro·pel·ler [prə·pel′ər] *n.* Blades turned by a motor to move a boat or an airplane through water or air: **Both boats stopped when their *propellers* got caught in a huge fishing net.**

Q

qui·et [kwī′ət] *adj.* Making no noise: **Kenji liked to play music and sing when the house seemed too *quiet*.** *syn.* silent

R

re·ceiv·er [ri·sē′vər] *n.* The part of the telephone that you hold to your ear: **No voice came from the *receiver* of the telephone, so Mom hung up.**

rec·og·nize [rek'əg·nīz'] *v.* To know or to tell apart: **Hector and Ramon could** *recognize* **their sister even though she was wearing a mask.**

reef [rēf] *n.* A ridge of sand, rocks, or coral, away from the shore but close to the water's surface: **Juana went swimming off the** *reef* **so she could look at the pretty tropical fish and sea plants.**

re·mind [re·mīnd'] *v.* **re·mind·ed, re·mind·ing** To help someone remember: **Alice** *reminded* **Benny which bus to take to her house even though he had already been there twice before.**

re·trieve [ri·trēv'] *v.* To get and bring back: **The dog liked to** *retrieve* **the branch and drop it at Sarah's feet every time she threw it.**

rig·ging [rig'ing] *n.* The ropes used to raise and hold the sails of a ship: **The first time we attached the sail to the** *rigging,* **we put it on upside down!**

route [rōot *or* rout] *n.* The way taken from one place to another: **The** *route* **of the school bus went past Carla's house.**

run·ner [run'ər] *n.* The long ski on the bottom of a sled used on snow and ice: **One** *runner* **on the bottom of the snow-mobile looked crooked.**

S

sal·vage [sal'vij] *n.* The act of saving something: **The team found many treasures during** *salvage* **of the sunken ship.**

scat·ter [skat'ər] *v.* To spread out into different places: **Every time I tried to read the paper, the wind would** *scatter* **it all over the yard, and I would have to gather it up again.**

scoff [skof *or* skôf] *v.* **scoffed, scoff·ing** To make fun of something that you think is silly or untrue: **People** *scoffed* **at Columbus when he said the earth was round, but he was right.**

recognize The word *recognize* has two main parts. *Re-* is a prefix that means "again" or "back." *Cognoscere*, a Latin word, means "to know." When you put the parts together, you can see that *recognize* means "to know again."

rigging

runner

a	add	o͞o	took
ā	ace	o͞o	pool
â	care	u	up
ä	palm	û	burn
e	end	yo͞o	fuse
ē	equal	oi	oil
i	it	ou	pout
ī	ice	ng	ring
o	odd	th	thin
ō	open	th	this
ô	order	zh	vision

ə = { a in *above*   e in *sicken*
       i in *possible*
       o in *melon*   u in *circus* }

shammy A *shammy* is a smooth polishing cloth first made from the skin of an antelope. This animal lives in the mountains of France and has the French name *chamois*. People who speak French say *chamois* as if it is spelled the same as *shammy*. People who speak English have begun to spell it s-h-a-m-m-y, according to the way it sounds. You may see it spelled both ways in books written in English.

shrug

snowmobile

shad·ow [shad′ō] *n.* The shade or darkness made by something blocking light: **Playing in the sunny yard, Clara tried to step on Paco's *shadow*.**

shal·low [shal′ō] *adj.* Not deep: **The water was so *shallow* that it only came up to our ankles.**

sham·my [sham′ē] *n.* A soft leather made from the skin of antelopes or other animals: **Sara always used a *shammy* to polish her car.**

sharp·shoot·er [shärp′shoo′tər] *n.* Someone with very good aim: **Candy was such a *sharpshooter* that she could make a basket from anywhere on the court.**

shrug [shrug] *v.* **shrugged, shrug·ging** To raise the shoulders to show that you aren't sure about something.

sledge [slej] *n.* A big sled used to move heavy loads over snow and ice: **The ranger put the injured skier on a *sledge* to move him to the hospital.**

slen·der [slen′dər] *adj.* Thin: **The trunks of young trees are very *slender* compared to the trunks of older trees.**

smol·der [smōl′dər] *v.* **smol·dered, smol·der·ing** To burn slowly, making smoke but no flame: **The fire *smoldered* after they thought it was out, and it burst into flame later.**

snow·mo·bile [snō′mō·bēl′] *n.* A small sled with a motor but no wheels that goes on snow: **We could drive the *snowmobile* when there was a lot of snow.**

spire [spīr] *n.* The pointed top of a building: **The lightning struck the *spire* of the town hall and knocked down the top half.**

spray [sprā] *n.* Tiny drops of water blowing in the air: **I love to sit in the front of the boat with the *spray* hitting my face and cooling me off.**

sprin·kle [spring′kəl] *v.* **sprin·kled, sprin·kling** To let fall in drops: *Sprinkling* the lawn is one of my jobs.

spy [spī] *v.* **spied, spy·ing** To see or catch sight of: **Mrs. Lopez *spied* the children running over the hill on their way home.**

stat·ue [stach′o͞o] *n.* Something made of clay, wood, metal, stone, or other material to look like a person or animal: **Lenora liked to make clay *statues* of cats in her art class.**

string [string] *v.* **strung, string·ing** To attach one or more strings to something: **As a joke, Maura *strung* Cassie's guitar with fishing wire instead of guitar string.**

sur·face [sûr′fis] *n.* The outside or top part of something: **The *surface* of the desk was smooth and shiny.**

sus·pect [sə·spekt′] *v.* **sus·pect·ed, sus·pect·ing** To think something is possible: ***Suspecting* that it might rain, Connie took her raincoat.**

swift [swift] *adj.* Very fast: **The waiter made a *swift* dive and caught the glass as it fell off the table.**

tal·on [tal′ən] *n.* The claw of a bird of prey: **The falcon swooped down and grabbed the field mouse in its sharp *talons*.**

taut [tôt] *adj.* Stretched tight: **Dad and I pulled the ropes *taut* so the tent would not fall down.**

ter·rain [tə·rān′] *n.* An area of land: **Since the *terrain* was rocky and dry, farmers would have a hard time growing crops there.**

ter·ri·fied [ter′ə·fīd] *adj.* Very scared: **Sally was *terrified* that she would forget her lines in the middle of the play.**

thong [thông] *n.* A thin strip of leather: **Campers often use a *thong* to tie things together because leather is very strong and easy to tie.**

thread [thred] *v.* **thread·ed, thread·ing** To wind through openings: **We saw our cousins *threading* their way through the crowd at the carnival.**

talon

a	add	o͞o	took
ā	ace	o͞o	pool
â	care	u	up
ä	palm	û	burn
e	end	yo͞o	fuse
ē	equal	oi	oil
i	it	ou	pout
ī	ice	ng	ring
o	odd	th	thin
ō	open	th	this
ô	order	zh	vision

ə = { a in *above*   e in *sicken*
 i in *possible*
 o in *melon*   u in *circus* }

tiller

unharness

vaudeville Six hundred years ago in France, there was a town called Vau-de-Vire. The people who lived there were famous for writing funny songs. Somehow, the name for these songs changed to *Vaudeville*. Americans borrowed this word and used it to mean a show made up of songs, dances, comedy, and even circus acts.

throt·tle [throt'(ə)l] *n.* A lever or pedal that helps an engine start and run: **He pulled on the *throttle* to start the boat.**

till·er [til'ər] *n.* A handle used to steer a boat: **Letting go of the *tiller* will make a boat spin in circles.**

tim·ber [tim'bər] *n.* A piece of wood: **The *timbers* of the ship had begun to rot, so the crew used new wood for the repairs.**

tow [tō] *v.* **towed, tow·ing** To pull with a rope or a chain: **Rob will watch while the tugboat is *towing* the big ship down the river.**

trans·late [trans·lāt'] *v.* To change words and sentences from one language into another: **Teresa could *translate* what her teacher said into Spanish so that her mother could understand it.**

tri·um·phant [trī·um'fənt] *adj.* Feeling thrilled and happy about winning: **The *triumphant* soccer team gave the trophy to the school principal after the game.**

U

un·con·trolled [un'kən·trōld'] *adj.* Out of control; without order or limits: **The *uncontrolled* floods could not be stopped, and they destroyed the farmland.**

un·har·ness [un·här'nis] *v.* **un·har·nessed, un·har·ness·ing** To unfasten or make free: **The farmer *unharnessed* the horses from the plow and let them go into the field.**

V

vau·de·ville [vôd'(ə·)vil *or* vōd'(ə·)vil] *n.* A show with many different acts: **The third-grade class put on an old-fashioned *vaudeville* show with many songs, jokes, and dances.**

ven·ture [ven'chər] *n.* Something to do that is somewhat dangerous and might not be successful: **The explorer's first *venture* into the jungle was a short hike to the river.**

vig·or·ous·ly [vig′ər·əs·lē] *adv.* With a great deal of energy: **Trent scrubbed the window** *vigorously* **to remove all the spots and dirt.**

wealth [welth] *n.* Riches or money: **The** *wealth* **of the king was far greater than any of his poor subjects.**

wel·come [wel′kəm] *v.* To greet someone.

with·er [with′ər] *v.* **with·ered, with·er·ing** To weaken and dry up: **After three weeks in the vase, the roses had** *withered* **away and were lifeless.**

wrig·gle [rig′əl] *v.* **wrig·gled, wrig·gling** To squirm or twist like a worm. *syn.* wiggle

vigorously

a	add	o͞o	took
ā	ace	o͞o	pool
â	care	u	up
ä	palm	û	burn
e	end	yo͞o	fuse
ē	equal	oi	oil
i	it	ou	pout
ī	ice	ng	ring
o	odd	th	thin
ō	open	th	this
ô	order	zh	vision

ə = { a in *above*   e in *sicken*
      i in *possible*
      o in *melon*   u in *circus* }

INDEX OF
TITLES AND AUTHORS

Page numbers in light print refer to information about the author.

Acknowledgments continued

Philomel Books: Owl Moon by Jane Yolen, illustrated by John Schoenherr. Text copyright © 1987 by Jane Yolen; illustrations copyright © 1987 by John Schoenherr. *Lon Po Po, A Red-Riding Hood Story from China* by Ed Young. Copyright © 1989 by Ed Young.

Price Stern Sloan Publishers, Inc., Los Angeles, CA: "Mysterious Treasure" from *50 Mysteries I Can Solve* by Susannah Brin and Nancy Sundquist. "Chocolate Chip Cookie Caper" from *50 Mysteries I Can Solve* by Susannah Brin and Nancy Sundquist, illustration by Neal Yamamoto.

G. P. Putnam's Sons: Cover illustration by Richard Williams from *Herbie Jones* by Suzy Kline. Copyright © 1985 by Suzy Kline.

Random House, Inc.: Cover illustration by Keith Kohler from *The Titanic: Lost . . . and Found* by Judy Donnelly. Illustration copyright © 1987 by Keith Kohler. Illustration from p. 62 by Arnold Lobel from *The Random House Book of Poetry for Children*, selected by Jack Prelutsky. Illustration copyright © 1983 by Random House, Inc.

Marian Reiner, on behalf of Myra Cohn Livingston: "Rain" from *A Song I Sang To You* by Myra Cohn Livingston. Text copyright © 1984, 1969, 1967, 1965, 1959, 1958 by Myra Cohn Livingston.

Scholastic, Inc.: Cover illustration by Meredith Johnson from *Rent a Third Grader* by B. B. Hiller. Illustration copyright © 1988 by Scholastic, Inc.

Simon & Schuster Books for Young Readers, a division of Simon & Schuster, Inc.: The Keeping Quilt by Patricia Polacco. Copyright © 1988 by Patricia Polacco.

Troll Associates: Cover illustration by Jean Helmer from *Amazing World of Night Creatures* by Janet Craig. Copyright © 1990 by Troll Associates.

Handwriting models in this program have been used with permission of the publisher, Zaner-Bloser, Inc.

Every effort has been made to locate the copyright holders for the selections in this work. The publisher would be pleased to receive information that would allow the correction of any omissions in future printings.

Photograph Credits

Key: (t) top, (b) bottom, (l) left, (r) right, (c) center.

UNIT 1

16, HBJ Photo; 31, Courtesy John Schoenherr; 32, HBJ Photo; 66–67, HBJ/Maria Paraskevas; 68–69, HBJ Photo; 72–73, HBJ Photo; 96, Courtesy Houghton Mifflin; 98–99, HBJ/Maria Paraskevas; 100, HBJ Photo; 120(t), Momatiuk/Eastcott/Woodfin Camp & Assoc.; 120(b), Caroline Povungnituk, *Untitled (Otter)*, © 1957, stone, 6.9 × 19.3 × 8.2 cm, The Swinton Collection, Gift of the Women's Committee, Ernest Mayer/Winnipeg Art Gallery; 121(t), S.J. Krasemann/Peter Arnold, Inc.; 121(c), Momatiuk/Eastcott/Woodfin Camp & Assoc.

UNIT 2

126, HBJ/Britt Runion; 128, HBJ Photo; 140–141, HBJ/Maria Paraskevas; 142–143, 144–145, 145(t), 146–147, 147(c), William Munoz, copyright 1990 by Holiday House, Inc. All rights reserved. Reprinted from YELLOWSTONE FIRES: FLAMES AND REBIRTH by permission of Holiday House; 148–149, Jim Peaco/National Park Service; 148(c), Ted Wood/Picture Group; 150–151, Ted Wood/Picture Group; 152–153, 152(c), 154–155, 155(c), William Munoz, copyright 1990 by Holiday House, Inc. All rights reserved. Reprinted from YELLOWSTONE FIRES: FLAMES AND REBIRTH by permission of Holiday House; 156–157, Pat & Tom Lesson/Photo Researchers; 157(c)–158(background), William Munoz, copyright 1990 by Holiday House, Inc. All rights reserved. Reprinted from YELLOWSTONE FIRES: FLAMES AND REBIRTH by permission of Holiday House; 158(c), Jim Tuton; 162, HBJ Photo; 174, Courtesy Sean Kernan/Putnam; 184, HBJ/Britt Runion; 204–205(background), HBJ Photo; 204(t)–205(t), HBJ/Gill Kenny for Black Star; 208(t), Tom McHugh/Photo Researchers; 209(t), Ancient Art & Architecture Collection.

UNIT 3

214–215, HBJ/Maria Paraskevas; 216–217, HBJ Photo; 217, HBJ Photo; 234, HBJ Photo; 235, HBJ Photo; 248–249, HBJ/Maria Paraskevas; 250–251, HBJ Photo; 270–271(background), NOTES ON THE LIFE AND WORKS OF BERNARD ROMANS by P. Lee Phillips, courtesy The University Presses of Florida, © 1975; 270(l), The Granger Collection; 271(t), Art Seitz/Gamma Liaison; 271(c), Jeffrey Cardenas/Sygma; 271(b), Kent Ancliffe; 276–277, HBJ Photo; 277, HBJ Photo; 296(t), AP/Wide World; 304–305, Nawrocki Stock Photo; 331, Steve Satushek/Image Bank; 334, Grafton M. Smith/Image Bank; 336, Stephen Derr/Image Bank; 337, Hans Wendler/Image Bank.

Illustration Credits

Key: (t) top, (b) bottom, (l) left, (r) right, (c) center.

Table of Contents Art

Tina Holdcroft, 5 (tr) (br), 7 (br), 8 (tl), 9 (br); Burton Morris, 4 (tl), 6–7 (c), 9 (tr); Tim Raglin, 4 (bl), 6 (tl) (bl), 8–9 (c); Peggy Tagel, 4–5 (c), 7 (tr), 8 (bl).

Unit Opening Patterns

Dan Thoner

Bookshelf Art

Gerald Bustamante, 212–213; David Diaz, 124–125; Randy Verougstraete, 12–13.

Theme Opening Art

Ray-Mel Cornelius, 207–208; Byron Gin, 214–215; Doug Henry, 14–15; Nathan Jarvis, 66–67; Anne Kennedy, 98–99; Mercedes McDonald, 274–275; Ross MacDonald, 160–161; San Murata, 126–127.

Theme Closing Art

Regan Dunnick, 159; Tuko Fujisaki, 119, 207; Peter Horjus, 303; Nathan Jarvis, 97; Dave Jonason, 183; Edward Martinez, 65; Clarence Porter, 247; Randy Verougstrate, 273.

Connections Art

Roseanne Litzinger, 120–121; David Diaz, 208–209.

Selection Art

Jim Arnosky, 32–45; Ken Brown, 298–302; Denise Brunkus, 186–203; Jim Campbell, 140–141; Mr. Amos Ferguson, 232–233; Stephen Gammell, 234–245; Manuel Garcia, 59–64; Ed Gazsi, 272; Gail Gibbons, 250–269; Jennifer Hewitson, 178–182; Dave Jonason, 183; Judy Labrasca, 100–117; Arnold Lobel, 118; Bill Peet, 68–96; Patricia Polacco, 216–231; Robert Rayevsky, 176, 177; Gordon Sauve, 206; John Schoenherr, 16–31; Ann Strugnell, 46–57; Chris Van Allsburg, 276–297; Beatriz Vidal, 128–139; Neal Yamamoto, 206; Ed Young, 162–173.